EMBRACING YOUR DARKNESS

AN INTUITIVE WOMAN'S GUIDE TO
EMPOWERMENT, HOLISTIC HEALING &
SPIRITUAL GROWTH THROUGH
SHADOW WORK

Y.D. GARDENS

THE EMERALD
S O C I E T Y

A SPECIAL GIFT TO MY READERS

Visit emeraldsocpublishing.com to download your FREE copy!

Hey lovely, why not jump in and join our tribe?

ALSO BY Y.D. GARDENS

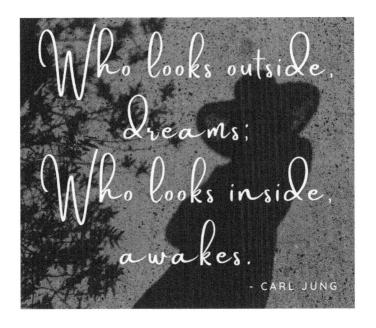

Growing Into You

Growing Stronger

Awakening to Authenticity Collection

The Well-Being Handbook

INTRODUCTION

> *One does not become enlightened by imagining figures of light, but by making the darkness conscious.*

— CARL G. JUNG

Meeting your Shadow is an alchemical process of transformation. Shadow Work, as it is commonly referred to, is a complex inner space journey that leads to living a full life as your most authentic self. The Shadow refers to the layers of your psyche that are often unrecognized or repressed; the myriad thoughts, emotions, and experiences that we subconsciously bury within the depths of our mind. That's right: We hide from our darkness, avoiding the parts of ourselves that are displeasing to our conscious mind.

Why do we do this?

Survival. To maintain our own self-preservation, we avoid facing the most sensitive and painful truths about who we are. We have this powerful ability to instinctively turn a blind eye to things we refuse to acknowledge about our own holistic being.

We assume that we know who we are, what our values are, and what defines us. But what if we are mistaken?

I can assure you that we are. Mistaken, that is. You see, until we are able to explore all facets of our being – including, most importantly, the tangled web formed by our shadow – we live under the illusion of being whole, defined by the image of ourselves that we choose to project onto the world. However, we are merely allowing a fraction of our true self to surface, burying what might evoke feelings of inadequacy, fear, and shame, to name only a few.

All these repressed thoughts, needs, and emotions cause inner decay. If you do not treat them as part of your whole entity, you can be sure they will resurface time and again. When ignored, these less desirable aspects create a slow, merely perceivable putrefaction within. This, sooner or later, permeates and affects all aspects of our lives.

Confronting your Shadow is the only way to decelerate or put a stop to this decay. Shadow work, exploring your inner demons and learning to accept and nurture all parts of your true self, is the key to liberation from trauma as well as holistic well-being. In the following pages, you'll learn more about your own Shadow and how to face it in order to become your most authentic, happiest self.

Now, let's begin by defining the Shadow. I like to imagine my own shadow as being a web of events that have triggered feelings, behaviors, and emotions that, for one reason or another, I deemed inappropriate or too painful to keep at the surface of my mind. For example, shameful childhood memories tend to lurk within the shadow web. In short, most negative aspects of the self are included in the Shadow. This means that elements of ourselves that we have rejected or deemed as 'bad' reside there.

As you can imagine, harboring these deep within ourselves will undoubtedly take a toll on our mental and emotional well-being. Where it really gets interesting, however, is when we begin to realize how this web of darkness affects our mindset and our relationships. All of us use a variety of defense mechanisms to avoid facing our darker truths. Many of us tend to project our Shadow onto others, meaning that we recognize our perceived inferiority in others as moral deficiencies.

For example, suppose being creative is something that is deemed as 'bad' by a child's parents, and the child receives disapproval when they are being creative. In that case, they are likely to incorporate creativity into their Shadow. As a result, they will frown upon, mock, or disapprove of other creative individuals. These types of defense mechanisms are used subconsciously and are considered as the emergence of the "dark side" of the personality.

Everyone has a Shadow self. What's more, your shadow can become your greatest ally. However, if it isn't dealt with consciously, it only grows darker.

Carl Gustav Jung's Contribution

In the discussion of Shadow Work, it is essential to introduce Carl G. Jung, a Swiss psychiatrist and the founder of analytical psychology. Interestingly, Sigmund Freud and Jung were friends, but their relationship ended early on due to disagreements in each other's doctrine. In fact, Jung criticized Freud for his emphasis on sexuality during development, arguing that it is not the main component of the psyche. Jung first talked about the Shadow as equivalent to the Freudian unconscious but expanded Freud's idea of it to include both the personal and the collective unconscious.

Now, to break it down, Jung's theory suggests that the psyche is composed of the ego, the personal unconscious, and the collective unconscious. As such, the ego is representative of the conscious mind. It is the active thinking we partake in continuously. Moreover, the ego is also a shield for the unconscious, meaning that it protects the conscious from the contents of the unconscious. It does this by automatically blocking any unpleasant or unwarranted thoughts and memories that might arise from the unconscious. In the following chapters, we will explore the mechanics of this phenomenon.

The personal unconscious includes the person's suppressed memories. These are usually traumatic memories that are hidden from the ego because they would cause tremendous pain that the ego wouldn't be able to handle. For instance, I might remember consciously (which means that I am able to recall the memory at any time) that when I was six years old, I fell from a swing and broke my arm. However, I might not consciously recall that my sister deliberately pushed me off the swing, as it is too traumatic for me to deal with the painful truth that she intended to hurt me. This part of the memory is suppressed and stored within the uncon-scious. This means that I am not able to recall it at will, but I might be able to do so after lots of inner-work, psychother-apy, and with the help of a professional.

Finally, as a third, the collective unconscious is the psychological inheritance of knowledge and experiences from our ancestors that we all share as a species (like the instinct of sex). The next section discussing archetypes will illustrate what the collective unconscious is.

Archetypes

The Archetypes are innate, universal, and hereditary models that organize our experiences (Jung, 1960). They are in the collective unconscious, meaning that everybody has their qualities, which are the same for everyone. However, the difference lies in how each of us expresses these archetypes or which ones are suppressed. For example, ethics originate from archetypes - they are almost innate in every one of us, are shared among all cultures, but different importance is placed among each culture. One culture values honesty more than, let's say, altruism.

Furthermore, in Jungian psychology, archetypes play an essential role in personality, and most people are dominated by one archetype. The four main archetypes are the Persona, the Shadow, the Anima or Animus, and the Self. Later in this book, we will look at more archetypes, but we'll stick with the basics for now. Let's have a brief look at these.

The Persona

The Persona is the way we present ourselves to others. It comprises the different 'masks' we wear in various social situations or groups. It protects the ego from negative self-images and various threats. It is formed during childhood when we are taught the appropriate behaviors that fit our social expectations and norms. The Persona's function is to limit our socially unacceptable primitive urges (like sexuality) and emotions (like revengefulness). Most of us have identified so much with the archetype that we have lost our true selves. Nevertheless, working with our psyche (Shadow Work is one way to do that) is a way to remember who we truly are.

The Shadow

What differentiates the Jungian Shadow from the Freudian unconscious is that the Shadow includes everything that isn't conscious, either positive or negative. Furthermore, the Shadow can appear in dreams or visions as a person of the same sex (von Franz, 1978). The first layers (which are usually evident in dreams) contain the flow and manifestations of personal experiences, underneath which are the archetypes. As part of the unconscious, it includes repressed ideas, desires, and instincts. However, it is important to stress that no part of the psyche is 'bad' or deliberately 'evil.' All parts of us, our psyches and even mental disorders, want to protect us from harm. In other words, they all do the best they can at any given moment, in the present situation. For instance, someone who is bullied at school may fall into depression and not have the energy to get out of bed or do anything else. This is the psyche's way of protecting this person from further harm by removing them from the situation that caused harm in the first place.

If my creativity as a child was deemed 'bad' by my parents, teacher, or the society I grew up in, then I will repress my creativity into my Shadow. I will do this so that I can survive in an environment that is 'hostile' to my true self and receive the maximum amount of acceptance, love, and care from my environment. I will do this to protect myself from the trauma of being rejected by important figures in my life. In other words, it is less harmful to my psyche to repress one part of me compared to being rejected or unloved. In that sense, the Shadow helps us adapt to social norms and expectations and build a socially acceptable Persona. It does this by containing, in a state of repression, things that are unacceptable to society or our own morality and values. For instance, if revengefulness is considered highly immoral in my environment, then I am more likely to repress any feelings or revengefulness I might have in the Shadow.

Jung theorized that encountering the Shadow is the key to individuation. This is a psychic process by which the self is differentiated from the unconscious throughout development. After the person has integrated innate elements of their personality, immature psyche components, and life experiences, the person functions as a whole. In other words, individuation means becoming your one true self. Moreover, it is the way to integrate the other elements of the psyche, including the Persona, the Shadow, and the Anima or Animus. With this process, the person confronts aspects of the self that they usually ignore because these aspects are difficult to accept. This ignorance leads to unconscious conflicts that cause problems in the conscious life. There are several stages to the individuation process, the second of which is to experience the Shadow. The breakdown of the Persona in the therapeutic process leads to the confrontation of the Shadow, with the aim to assimilate it into the ego.

The Anima or Animus

These are the masculine and feminine forms of the same word. The Anima is the feminine image in the male psyche, and the Animus is the masculine image of the female psyche (Cherry, 2020). It is essential to mention that this has nothing to do with the person's gender or sex. The Anima/Animus is our "true self" and the primary source of communication with the collective unconscious. These images are formed by the content of both the personal and collective unconscious. For instance, the collective unconscious contains ideas about how women should behave. The personal unconscious has formed unique images of women based on experiences with important female figures (like mothers, sisters, wives, etc.). To encounter and work with this archetype, you need to have worked on breaking down the Persona and acknowledging the Shadow. Integrating this archetype is the third and final step to individuation.

The Self

This archetype represents the unification of both the person's conscious and unconscious. This can be achieved through the individuation process. The Self is the center of the whole personality, while the ego is the center of the conscious personality. In other words, you think your personality is the ego, but this only encompasses what you consciously know about yourself. On the other hand, the Self includes both that and everything that is unconscious (like the Shadow, the Anima/Animus, etc.).

Benefits of Shadow Work

People tend to look at their strengths and praise themselves for their accomplishments, which is much needed and very useful. However, in order to move forward, grow, and stop repeating the same mistakes, Shadow Work is essential. Looking at the deepest, darkest, most repressed sides of ourselves is a challenging process, albeit a very rewarding one. In other words, Shadow Work gives you the ground-breaking opportunity to begin your life anew and heal your past wounds. Shadow Work is a shame-free place to explore your inner space. It is important to remember that different parts of your life have different shadows, which need to be dealt with in relation to specific situations and desired outcomes. In this book, you will learn how to tackle the obstacles to embracing your shadow and sitting comfortably and confidently within your inner space. Here, you will also find ways to prepare yourself to begin this process.

To begin with, Shadow Work helps you improve your relationships by enabling you to see yourself more clearly. This means that you are able to accept other people's Shadows, and their actions won't trigger you that easily, while you'll be communicating better with them. Moreover, your perception will become clearer, meaning that you'll be able to see yourself and others for who they are and become your authentic self at the same time. This will enable you to realistically assess and perceive yourself as neither too big nor too small. Your judgment will also be clearer when you're assessing your environment. Another benefit of Shadow Work is enhanced energy and improved physical health. Repressing parts of yourself as a means of self-protection and self-preservation requires immense amounts of energy. This concentrated energy can lead to physical pain, disease, fatigue, and lethargy, which can be dealt with by building inner strength and creating a sense of balance through Shadow Work.

Additionally, you can achieve psychological integration and maturity through the sense of wholeness and maturity that Shadow Work offers you. You can also develop greater creativity by unlocking your creative potential.

So, now that we know what the Shadow, Carl Jung, and Shadow Work are, it is time to utilize this knowledge and put it into perspective in the next chapter. There, we will cover the basics: how the Shadow is formed, how to identify it, the factors that feed it, and the impacts of thought and memory suppression. Creating your safe space is also a part of the foundation of Shadow Work, so we will explore tools to build a mental space for you to safely and wholly embark upon this process.

Let's begin.

1

SHADOW

The Origins of the Shadow

To begin with, we are born with a complete personality, expressing our true selves all the time without being censored. Growing up, we are taught by our environment (parents, teachers, and society) that not all parts of our personality are acceptable. Therefore, we feel the need to discard our 'bad' qualities by repressing them.

The 'bad' things are the first to be discarded, such as anger, jealousy, envy, parts of sexuality, or revengefulness. This happens by receiving negative cues from our environment (like punishment or disapproval), threatening our primary needs, like the need to be loved (Jeffrey, 2014a). So, in order to fulfill these needs, we needed to reject everything that was deemed unacceptable. This process is likely to discard 'good' qualities, like self-esteem, a sense of wholeness, intimacy, creativity, or playfulness. So, generally speaking, the shadow contains anything that has been repressed or denied.

Now, this is important: These qualities usually show up when we are annoyed at other people's qualities. For example, if someone's shadow includes the quality of self-righteousness, then this person will be annoyed at self-righteous people or notice them more compared to other people. This phenomenon is called 'projection' and works by detecting a quality in others so as to avoid noticing it within ourselves.

Furthermore, 'good' qualities that are included in the shadow might stand out in others (Barry & Blandford, n.d.). This means that we admire other people who possess the 'good' qualities we've incorporated in our shadow and exaggerate these characteristics on them. This, too, is projection. For instance, if someone's shadow includes spontaneity, this person will tend to admire others who are spontaneous. Nevertheless, the qualities of the shadow can emerge in everyday life. They are evident in spontaneous behaviors that "just happen." These are indicative of the qualities in the shadow that the person doesn't want to admit they are part of, usually through a fair amount of well-embedded denial. For example, if someone thinks that anger is unacceptable, then they might develop a flash temper and be triggered more easily. This denial doesn't allow the person to see or acknowledge the behavior when they're doing it. This means that the Shadow operates without our control (Jeffrey, 2014).

How to Spot the Shadow

There are a few ways to get to know the qualities of your shadow.

The first thing you can do is observe the qualities that annoy you or those you admire in others. Recognizing that you are projecting your shadow qualities onto others is the first step to getting to know the contents of your shadow.

Try to notice the following and think of the reasons why they happen:

a) Who you attack repeatedly.

b) Who always rubs you the wrong way.

c) With whom you have continual tension.

d) Who you try to avoid.

Try to notice which behaviors are in control of you. These are spontaneous behaviors or reactions that you can't control and tend to "just happen" when you're triggered. They can also be behaviors that you later regret. These can be compulsive behaviors (things you feel like you have to do, no matter what), bad habits, and patterns of thought that take over. They indicate that some part of you isn't integrated and hides in the shadow.

Notice the following:

- Which emotions constantly nag you, even if you try your best to suppress them.
- Reactions that are out of proportion.
- The cases in which you feel emotionally numb.

When our Shadow is unrecognized, it can cause self-sabotage. Some common patterns of self-sabotage are:

- Feeling tired for no reason.
- Spending a lot of time on social media without understanding why.
- Feeling that you have creative potential, yet being unable to do anything with it or don't know what exactly it is.
- Making decisions that go against your best interests or your long-term plans.

Notice your dreams. Psychoanalysis suggests that dreams reflect the contents of the unconscious and are therefore tools to explore it. The contents of the unconscious can appear in dreams as memories, people, emotions, or symbols.

*A*s I said before, the Shadow usually appears as a person of the same sex as the dreamer. It is important to analyze and observe the dreamer's interactions with the Shadow. For example, having a conversation with an aspect of the Shadow indicates that you're concerned with conflicting desires or intentions. Moreover, identification with a person you despise may mean that you haven't acknowledged a difference with this person, meaning that you might be rejecting some qualities of yourself (von Franz, 1978). For instance, if I dream about identifying with a self-righteous person I don't like, then self-righteousness might be a quality that I have, but I have rejected it and repressed it in my Shadow.

Shadow Work

As I said before, Carl Jung theorized that Shadow Work (as part of individuation) would lead to the liberation of the mind and the body. It also helps you act out of purpose rather than being led or controlled by your darkness. The goal of Shadow Work is to get to know the Shadow, not to identify with it. Identifying completely with the Shadow means that you can fall victim to it and, ultimately, merge with it. Merging with the Shadow is when the person's actions are affected mainly by their Shadow. Shadow possession leads to falling into your own traps, self-sabotage, lack of purpose, lack of creativity, and being extremely reactive, among others.

The Four Quarters of Shadow Work

With that said, it is theorized that there are four quarters in Shadow Work. These are walls in the pyramid of the Shadow Workroom that are associated with the four elements in astrology or the primary emotions that people feel, among other things. The walls are energies or archetypes that contain basic, ancient instincts, which all of us repress in our effort to be part of our organized society. The Quarters help identify and process the Shadow. The process of repression happens due to traumas created by our environment while growing up, and consequently, we put them in the Shadow. In other words, we are shamed for these instincts and taught that these energies are unacceptable. When these energies are in the Shadow, we usually appear as having too much or too little of them.

Carl Jung saw these energies as fundamental units of the human mind and called them 'archetypes' (Jeffrey, 2017a). He theorized that they are structures of reactions that frame our lives. They can be found in religions, legends, myths, and even dreams, fantasies, and behavior. They also tend to influence the relationships we have with others and ourselves. Archetypes reside in the unconscious and influence us without us knowing, and they are said to be more than 250 in number. In that, they influence our behaviors by assuming the form of instincts. These biological urges activate pre-existing patterns of behavior which are shared by all humanity. For instance, when the archetype of the Hero is triggered, we become more brave, persistent, and run to action. Different archetypes also trigger different emotions, meaning that the emotions we experience are the emotions of archetypes. For example, courage is associated with the Warrior archetype. In addition, by tapping into our emotions, we add a sense of meaning to our lives.

The Magician

The Magician's energy belongs in the west, is associated with air (and air zodiac signs), and it aims at generating options for us, guiding us through detachment, and giving us perspective. The Magician isn't so much concerned with morality or what is good and bad. Accessing this energy means detaching yourself from the situation and seeing what you can get from it. In addition, it is an elder or adviser energy (such as Merlin, in mythology). In real life, the Magician can be a therapist or a person who can help us get perspective. All archetypes have a feminine and a masculine side, which has nothing to do with the person's actual gender or sex. Men and women have both a feminine and a masculine side in Jungian psychology, and the goal is to achieve a balance between them. With that said, the masculine side of the Magician is living life by following a model (like cooking with a recipe). On the other hand, the feminine magician comes from the intuitive side (like cooking by taste). This is usually manifested as going into a situation and feeling it so that you can decide what to do next.

*I*nside the family system, the Magician is usually the Clown, Mascot, or Trickster energy, meaning that this person can detach from a situation easily and make a joke, even in difficult situations. The gateway emotion to the Magician is fear. This means that feeling your fear and welcoming it opens up the Magician energy. The animal instincts included in the Magician are those associated with territory, bonding, being the alpha male or female, and the predatory instincts, in general. This innate instinct that we all have is rejected by society. Therefore, it goes into the Shadow and can show density (like lacking perspective or insight) when we have too little. On the contrary, when we have too much, it sparks confusion, such as not being able to keep up with our options or too many things going on in our heads at once. The Magician is usually put into Shadow by internalizing the shame created from feeling like you're bad. This, in turn, creates trauma.

. . .

The Sovereign

This is the King or Queen. It belongs in the north and is associated with fire. The energy of the Sovereign has to do with the dream, mission, and the motivation to achieve the dream. The masculine side (King) can see the mission and outline the dream. The feminine side (Queen) will nurture, motivate, and empower the mission. This type of energy is very much concerned about morality as well as right and wrong, making the Sovereign emotionally connected. It is also associated with self-esteem. In real life, the Sovereign can be a parent, a leader, or a person who guides other people in a direction. In a family setting, this person is the hero, little parent, or caretaker. They usually are the ones to get good grades and achieve goals while striving for perfection. In stressful situations, this kid will take over the role of the parent and take care of their siblings if needed.

Additionally, the gateway emotion to the Sovereign energy is joy. When we are happiest, we are also motivated to dream and achieve our goals, thus accessing the Sovereign energy. The animal instinct associated with this energy is the alpha male or female. As humans, we have the instincts to either be the alpha (or the leader) or follow the alpha. The Sovereign is often put in the Shadow because of being put down when trying to be the leader. When we have too little of this energy, we are shy (avoiding doing things, lacking motivation). When we have too much of it, we are shining (believing we can do everything, looking for love through displaying grandiosity). The unmet need is believing you're not good enough and thus trying to prove your worth by being perfect. This unmet need comes from the trauma of conditional love (being loved for what we do, instead of who we are).

he Lover

The Lover energy is placed in the direction of the east and is associated with water and the water signs. This energy has to do with connection through feeling and sexuality. It is all about connecting with ourselves and others and is where the Inner Child lives. Moreover, the masculine side seeks to connect through the spirit, and the feminine side aims to connect through the soul. In real life, artists model this type of energy. In the family context, it is the very quiet, intense, artistic child who spends time alone. This is called the "lost child" who is intuitively connected with the rest of the family. The gateway emotion to the Lover energy is grief.

Furthermore, the animal instinct associated with this energy is bonding. When in Shadow, the Lover will either be too stoic and won't be able to show vulnerability (too little energy) or overflowing, acting out all the time, and the emotions are taking over the person (too much energy). Addictions and compulsive behaviors are most commonly observed when there is an imbalance of the Lover energy. The main message associated with the Lover energy, when it is in the Shadow, is believing you don't love right.

. . .

The Warrior

The Warrior energy is placed in the south and is associated with earth and the earth signs. This energy has to do with power and accomplishments through personal boundaries, either by expanding them or restricting them. Its masculine side is associated with offense and carries out' operations'. It expands the boundaries of the personal realm. The feminine side wants to defend personal boundaries when attacked. This energy is interconnected with the Magician, the Sovereign, and the Lover. The Magician sees the options, the Sovereign considers this option to be a vision, the Lover puts a deep feeling to it and empowers it, and the Warrior carries the whole thing out.

Moreover, the Warrior is altruistic energy that is willing to do something hard if it benefits the greater good. In real life, the Warrior energy is embodied by lawyers, police officers, judges, and business people. In a family system, a child with a lot of Warrior energy would be the rebel or the scapegoat because they always break family rules or take the blame and get punished.

Since this type of energy is all about personal space and boundaries, it is associated with the animal instinct of territoriality (owning territory and defending it). This territory is the ego. Furthermore, the gateway emotion to accessing the Warrior energy is anger because people are usually angry when their boundaries are being overstepped. In that, bitterness is usually expressed in the body through pain. In terms of Shadow Warrior, a person with too little Warrior energy can be a victim by not having firm boundaries, not being able to say no, putting themselves second, and hating conflict. Someone with too much of it will be very defensive, attacking others and not letting people in. The Shadow Warrior can be created by the message that you don't exist apart from others. This means this person feels like they're not separate from others and that the boundaries around their ego are not clear. This trauma is created when the person's boundaries are continuously overstepped while not being allowed to have their own thoughts, dreams, actions, and space.

The Container

Shadow Work can help you recognize hidden qualities and bring them to light by creating a safe space to explore these energies. Finding the wisdom hidden in the Shadow will help you use it in your life. Essentially, the Container is a safe space in your psyche, where you can explore the Shadow and work with its energies. This will make you feel like you're in control of your life rather than being controlled by your Shadow. The container aims to act these energies out in a safe place and learn how to manage them outside of it. A safe container offers secure space for Shadow Work.

The container includes several things, like:

1. What you want to see happen in this process.
   These can be your goals (for example, wanting to control your anger if you have anger issues). You are responsible for choosing which qualities of the Shadow you want to work on and the depth you

want to reach. This is because you must work at your own pace and not be forced to face something you're not ready to face.

2. Safety to work on these qualities before you apply them to your life. You can learn how to handle and harness them so that they work better in your real life.

3. The Four Quarters we talked about previously. In the process of Shadow Work, it is important to work with the quarter you have too little of and bring it to the forefront. That is because seeming to have too much of one energy is usually an effort to bring balance because you have too little of another.

*M*oreover, it is essential to know the role each archetype plays in the container.

1. The Magician holds the container. To integrate the Magician, we use the Split. This tool helps you detach from the situation you're in to gain some perspective and, ultimately, bring the magician out of the Shadow.

2. The Sovereign fills the container with hopes and dreams. It can be balanced by getting support or blessing from an ideal figure and unconditional love.

3. The Lover helps you bond with your Inner Child. It can be balanced by working with the body. The

person observes their body and uses a technique called "the Switch" to refrain from what is happening to the body and how the person feels about it.

4. The Warrior helps you protect yourself, your boundaries, and your container's boundaries. It can be balanced by setting boundaries. These can be in the future (as goals) or in the present (as a physical boundary that gives room to the person to feel their Warrior energy and express it in a way that neither they nor anybody else gets hurt). It is important to remember that we put our Warrior energy in Shadow if we have hurt someone else with it in the past, or we saw someone get hurt by someone else's Warrior energy.

The Process of Shadow Work

Once you have recognized that you have a Shadow and that it contains many unpleasant things about yourself (and you still want to face it), the first thing you need to do is build a Container so that the process of Shadow Work is safe. After you decide what you want to see happen and what changes you'd like to make, you can combine the options.

In this process, it is essential to familiarize yourself with the four archetypes discussed above and try to see which ones you have too little or too much of in order to start working on balancing them. Remember that the Container is symbolic and represents the personality. It is a safe space where you can explore yourself without judgment or fear. After some time working with it, using the Container becomes an automatic pattern, meaning that you won't have to go back and remember the things you've put in there. In other words, once you have started exploring yourself, you can't go back and forget what you've learned. For instance, if you come to discover that you are too stoic and therefore have too little Lover energy, you can't simply pretend that you are unaware of this fact.

In this chapter, you learned all about the origins of your Shadow, how to spot it, the Container and its Four Quarters, as well as the process of Shadow Work. In Chapter 2, we will learn how to prepare ourselves before beginning Shadow Work by developing our self-awareness, learning about our Shadow type, and reaching out to our wounded Inner Child.

2

THE DARKNESS WITHIN

 In the midst of darkness, light persists.

— MAHATMA GANDHI

*A*s I've mentioned previously, the first step to Shadow Work is clarifying which outcomes you will be working towards in this process. Are you looking to tap into your true self? Perhaps to bring on personal growth? To change some of the things that are bothering you (like low self-esteem)? Even though Shadow Work can lead us in unexpected directions, having a general idea of what you want to achieve will give you some strength to power through during the more challenging parts of this process.

In the following pages, we will talk about getting to know your Shadow and how to begin the process of Shadow Work.

Self-awareness

To understand and encounter your Shadow, you need to know yourself first. In the shrine of the oracle Pythia at Delphi, one can find the inscription "γνῶθι σεαυτόν", which means "know thyself". But what does it mean to know yourself? Well, it implies knowing why you behave the way you do, what drives your decisions, and how you feel about yourself and those around you. In Shadow Work, self-awareness is both a prerequisite and an outcome, meaning that in order to start this process, you need to know about yourself, but when you finish, you'll know even more. In general, self-awareness is knowing what happens around you and what you're experiencing (Jeffrey, 2019). It is also knowing what you are doing and why. Nevertheless, Jungian psychology says that the contents of the unconscious often drive our behavior and actions. So, even if we choose and are aware of most of our actions and behaviors, the reasons or motives are sometimes unconscious. Furthermore, self-awareness is a skill that helps us grow and develop.

The first stage of learning this skill is unconscious incompetence. This means that when you start learning something, you are not aware of how poor you are at it, which can create discomfort. In other words, when you begin developing self-awareness, you can't see how much you don't know about yourself. After some time, you might realize that there is a lot you don't know about yourself, and this can cause discomfort. This can make you avoid the process or abandon it. However, you should trust the process and keep in mind that, in the end, it will definitely be worth it. So, for this reason, people go through life without self-awareness, as they're not willing to take the pain or discomfort associated with it. With the right tools, determination, and consistency, you can achieve it. Most people fail to develop their self-awareness because they tend to focus on changing their thoughts, beliefs, and biases and forget to include their emotions and instincts in the factors that drive their behavior. Here you'll find some activities that can help you get to know your personality:

- Personality tests. These are questionnaire-type tests that reveal your dominant behavior patterns and personality type. The Enneagram and the Myers-Briggs are two tests you can find online.

- Strengths assessment. These tests serve to identify your strengths and weaknesses, like the Values in Action Strength Test from the University of Pennsylvania.

- Self-reflection. This means taking time to reflect on your behavior each day. You can answer questions like "How do I perceive myself?", "How do others perceive me?" and "What can I learn about my behavior?".

- Personal values. Knowing your personal values helps you evaluate if your life is in accordance with them. Think about what is most important to you.

- Personal vision. Think about your ideal future self. This reflects how much of your innate potential you've realized. Clarifying your vision of the future will give you a sense of destiny.

- Journaling. Writing your thoughts and feelings down will help you objectify them and identify repeating patterns of behaviors and thoughts that are harmful to you.

- Personal narrative. This is your life story and ultimately a significant component of your personality. The story you tell yourself about your life reflects your personality. You can write down your life story and try to observe repeating patterns.

- Inner dialogue. Your inner voices have their own thoughts, feelings, and behaviors. Discussing with them will help you develop your self-awareness.

- Observe others. This is especially important in Shadow Work. It can help you observe what is bothering you and think critically about it.

Identifying your Shadow

Once you've established your goals, you need to identify which qualities your Shadow contains. To do this, you will first need to observe yourself. When are you triggered? What bothers you in others? If you can learn to pinpoint your triggers (as unpleasant as these realizations often are) by observing your thoughts towards others, you will be able to begin assembling the puzzle that is your Shadow. In short, I will show you how to notice when you're projecting your Shadow onto others and how being conscious of these projections will enable you to piece together your shadow self. This work is nonlinear; as we evolve throughout life, shaped by experiences, we use these tools to help us on our path to personal growth and peace of mind. Essentially, this means that you need to develop knowledge about yourself, for better and for worse. This is also the key to preventing resistance and changing a fixed mindset, which we'll talk about that in later chapters. In the discussion of self-awareness, the 12 Shadow types are central. These are 12 innate tendencies that form our personalities, depending on which ones we favor and which ones we avoid (Shadow Work Seminars, 2021). Furthermore, the 12 Shadow types give us information about our core traumas, main coping strategies, tendencies for imbalance, and self-concept. This is a great way to get to know your Shadow and yourself better.

. . .

The Magician Archetype

Since the Magician is all about perspective, it is characterized by the quality of Awareness. In that, the Detacher is a person who is good at stepping back and gaining perspective on people and situations. They weigh the situation before acting. They are usually introverts and prefer solitude. They can be with other people but need time to recharge afterward. They experience their emotions through their intellect rather than their body while avoiding emotional intensity. Although they're knowledgeable and independent, they often seem cool, aloof, and distant. People whose primary type is the Detacher carry the core trauma of being 'bad'. Therefore, the fear of being bad makes them avoid exposing whatever they consider to be 'bad' inside them. Detachers tend to have an active mental life as a means of controlling everything they deem inferior or inadequate within themselves and preventing it from coming out spontaneously through the expression of emotions. The Detacher has the Lover archetype in Shadow. What they have trouble recognizing and admitting is that they are actually emotional beings - and the fact that this is okay.

Secondly, there is the Optionizer. These people consider all the options before making a decision and are able to see many perspectives. They can also see many points of view in different situations. Moreover, they love to discover new possibilities but have difficulty deciding on one. In other words, decisions don't bring them a sense of relief or balance.

On the contrary, making a choice makes them feel restricted and like they have lost other, better opportunities. This can lead to procrastination and avoidance of making decisions. The core trauma of this type originates in having had to make a massive decision at an early age (such as choosing between two divorcing parents). This means that when they have to make a decision, they feel paralyzed and fear that their choice will bring negative results. When the Optionizer is one's primary type, the Warrior archetype is likely to reside in Shadow. To tap into their Warrior energy, Optionizers need to recognize and acknowledge their decisional making power as a privilege, no matter the possible outcomes.

The last type of this archetype is the Alerter. These people are very aware of possible threats and dangers. Alerters have a clear intellect and strong powers of perception, meaning that they tend to see things others miss. They can think critically and question things that seem suspicious or cynical. They are also skeptics who warn others about dangers and always question authority, which makes them unlikely to assume positions of power themselves. Alerters have the core trauma that they are bad and that something is wrong with them. They believe that if something is wrong with them, then something is wrong with others too and, therefore, need to guard themselves against others and themselves.

Consequently, they strive to create a sense of safety for themselves and others. Generally, others think that Alerters are very negative in actions, words, and thoughts; however, it is actually their effort to protect themselves and others from threats. If an Alerter becomes conscious of these patterns and their origin, they will stop feeling shame for the criticism they receive from others and, ultimately, understand that they aren't bad. Finally, the Sovereign archetype is in Shadow, and Alerters should tap into their Sovereign energy in order to access the good qualities of their Shadow (the 'gold').

. . .

he Sovereign Archetype

Since the Sovereign is all about perspective, it is characterized by the quality of Positivity. The first type is the Idealizer, who sees a world full of opportunities and has a lot of ideas. They usually take on leadership roles because they imagine how to make the world a better place and want to contribute to the world. They are lively, bright, and optimistic and tend to see the sunny side of things. On the other hand, their optimism makes them not want to look at problems and not deal with negative emotions. Instead, they want to see the positive in themselves and the situations they're in. This makes them avoid commitment and not fulfill their promises. The core trauma of people in this category is that they believe they aren't good enough. That is why they always want to be better than they are and, in turn, tend to perceive others as better than they actually are. They feel they need to keep expanding into bigger ideas, visions and see life in an ideal light. The Idealizers have their Warrior archetype in Shadow. To tap into their Warrior energy, they will need to set boundaries around their tendency to expand so as to protect their freedom and vulnerability.

Secondly, there is the Affecter. Affecters are deeply concerned about how others see them. They strive to impress with their capabilities and achievements and often succeed in impressing. They are usually competent and accomplished and have a high sense of mission. This makes them goal-oriented, motivated, and hardworking, to the point that they may appear to be workaholics. They also strive for excellence, and others usually praise and recognize them, to the extent where others might question whether the Affecters are genuine. They highly value recognition, which incites them to take up challenges to prove themselves. Like the Idealizers, the Affecters have the core trauma of believing they aren't good enough. To cope with this wound, they continually attempt to earn people's love to show the world that they are, in fact, enough. This is a never-ending cycle, where they keep trying to prove themselves over their lives. The Lover archetype is usually in Shadow. To tap into the Lover energy, they need to accept and appreciate their vulnerability and recognize that they are good enough as they are.

The third type is the Fosterer. Helping others and taking care of them through material or emotional assistance is what the Fosterers do. They usually play the role of the mother, father, or teacher to people, which means that others seek warmth, support, and nourishment from them. Consequently, the Fosterers often hold professional positions of power and positions that require taking responsibility for others. They also form relationships with others by empowering them but, at times, might seem smothering and somewhat manipulative. Again, as per the previous two types, they have the deep trauma of not being good enough. To compensate for this feeling of inadequacy, the Fosterers give much to others, which temporarily makes them feel like they are enough.

Furthermore, they give more than they take without realizing it. This draining cycle can also foster a victim/martyr mentality. Fosterers can learn to tap into their Magician energy to find more balance. This will enable them to gain a clearer image of themselves, which will also allow for a clearer perception of others.

.   .   .

The Warrior Archetype

Since the Warrior is all about taking action, setting boundaries, and asserting power, it is characterized by the quality of being Real. The first type in this category is the Upholder. Upholding means supporting, maintaining, and defending the standards of what is good and bad that we learned during early childhood. We all learned this through our caregivers' reactions to situations (approval or praise means that something is good, whereas punishment or disapproval implies that it is bad). Nevertheless, the Upholders will hold themselves more strongly to their standards than others. Upholding is, thus, a dominant feature of their personality, meaning that they have a heightened sense of right and wrong. Furthermore, their thinking is more binary (something is either good or bad, and there is nothing in between). All these can make them seem obsessive or fanatical.

The core trauma of these people has to do with sharp criticism, high standards, or enduring a hardship that they perceived as punishment in early childhood. Upholders believe that they will only be accepted if they do 'right', and that something terrible will happen to them if they do wrong. This means that they are always aware of the rules and the correct behavior as a precaution to avoid criticism or pain. Their whole life revolves around holding themselves to these standards, as well as those around them (who, by affiliation, these Warriors consider an extension of themselves). Consequently, the Upholders have a strong sense of duty and purpose. Openness, spontaneity, vulnerability, and dependency are all in Shadow, along with the Lover energy. They don't like these qualities due to the risk they pose of doing something wrong accidentally and thus being criticized. To tap into their Lover energy, they must learn to accept child-like qualities in themselves and others. As a result, they will be able to include in their standards of being 'good' the values of joy, vulnerability, and connection.

The next type is the Contester. People of this type need to challenge the validity of things constantly. They also need to push against people or situations to test their limits and measure themselves. This enables all of us to build boundaries around ourselves and declare our territory during early childhood. However, the Contesters might seem aggressive or intimidating to others. On that note, they have probably experienced something during childhood that came to disrupt this process of building boundaries and, by extension, to their self-building process. This means they have the core trauma of being unsure about their identity and believing that they don't matter. That is why they compete, push limits, and assert boundaries – at times recklessly. The Magician energy is in Shadow, which means that they need to learn to take an objective stance and see their vulnerable side.

The final type in this category is the Establisher. This is a person who establishes themselves as a distinct individual, which is key to their personality. We all go through this process around the age of two, when we realize who we are and that we are separate from other people. These people are more concerned about defining who they are and being unique. Standing out and being special is a crucial need for them, and it often leads to them being lonely. In groups, they perceive themselves as unique or rebellious and always find a way to distinguish themselves. Moreover, they don't conform. To build an identity, they strive to be successful in order to feel unique. On the other hand, this can make them seem self-centered and status-seeking.

. . .

The Lover Archetype

This archetype is about our childlike nature, like being spontaneous, emotional, and vulnerable. This category is characterized by the quality of being Open. The first type is the Relyer. These people depend on others due to being vulnerable and having a powerful longing for connection and belonging. To fulfill this need, they usually take care of others and give to them, to the point where they sacrifice their own boundaries. They prefer to depend on others rather than others depending on them. They can easily elicit help from people and value the powerful bonds they create with others because of their dependency.

Moreover, their core trauma is that they don't love right or that they aren't a loving person. As a result, they go to great lengths to build and maintain relationships through having others help them or give to them. For these people, the Warrior energy is usually in Shadow, which means that they need to learn how to set boundaries in their relationships by realizing that becoming self-sufficient and asserting themselves will lead them to strengthen their bonds with others.

The second type is the Yielder. People of this type surrender to unpleasant or difficult situations. In other words, they passively accept difficult situations rather than make things happen. They don't deny or run away from difficulties and can endure more hardships than other people. They submit to what is happening to them more easily, without reacting or trying to change it, seeming like they're not motivated and passive. When in groups, they are often the ones to take on the tasks no one else wants. Like the Relyers, the Yielders have the core trauma of believing that they don't love right or that they're not loving. That is why they act in ways that look like love. It is possible that, during early childhood, they have faced a situation that they couldn't change. They believe that love is surrendering to others in painful ways or assuming the role of the victim. Furthermore, the Sovereign archetype is in Shadow, meaning that they need to regain the hope they've lost due to being the victim and assume leadership in order to tap into this energy.

The last type in this category is the Releaser. Releasers allow whatever they're feeling to come out spontaneously, whether it is impulses, saying what they are thinking, or releasing emotions. They express their inner experiences and are spontaneous. Consequently, they tend to be creative, individualistic, highly emotional, and draw attention to themselves in groups. They are often melodramatic or develop addictions. The core trauma these people carry is that they aren't loving people. This means that they are emotional and expressive to compensate for this wound and prove that they can love. Furthermore, the Magician archetype is in Shadow, which means that they need to learn to step back and gain perspective on their emotions in order to tap into this energy.

Identifying your Wounded Inner Child

The Inner Child is our childlike aspect, and it includes what we learned as children and traumas during our childhoods. Observing and recognizing our traumas can lead us to our Inner Child.

Traumas are unspoken or unmet needs that create emotions, behaviors, and thoughts in the unconscious. They are usually related to fear, abandonment, rejection, shame, and helplessness we have experienced. These traumas can be major or minor, multilayered, or multigenerational. When we are traumatized, we lock away parts of ourselves in order to protect them – self-preservation. As such, when our Inner Child is triggered and old wounds are awakened, we can become vulnerable, unstable, and scared. When this happens, most of us tend to avoid the voice of our Inner Child instead of allowing ourselves to feel it. Reconnecting with our Inner Child will enable us to acknowledge our experiences, receive guidance, and open up to our most vulnerable experiences or major traumas in order to restore our inner peace. What we must learn to do is give our Inner Child permission to be, permission to hurt, and thus begin to heal. It's all about forgiving ourselves and creating healthy connections with others – but more on that in Chapter 6.

In this chapter, you learned tips about raising your self-awareness, the 12 Shadow types, and have had a peek into the importance of Inner Child work. In Chapter 3, we will talk about *The Work* by Byron Katie, which is a very powerful tool for anyone embarking on a self-healing journey. It is a straightforward approach, which makes it even more valuable. Utilizing this tool will allow you to get to know some aspects of your Shadow.

3

JOURNEY THROUGH INNER SPACE

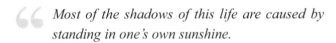

Most of the shadows of this life are caused by standing in one's own sunshine.

— RALPH WALDO EMERSON

*B*yron Katie is an American author and speaker who, since 2003, has been sharing with the world her approach titled "The Work." Her teachings on integrating the Shadow are profound and life-changing. Her approach is all about embracing yourself as whole, making peace with yourself, and accepting things as they are. Her approach can also help with destructive habits such as self-sabotage, negative thinking, and low self-worth. We will begin this chapter by tackling these issues, after which I will outline Byron Katie's groundbreaking approach. If you are not yet familiar with her work, you are in for quite a treat.

As discussed previously, many destructive habits are

formed through repressed elements residing in the Shadow. Self-sabotage is one common tool we use as a means of protecting ourselves. But does it actually help us?

Self-sabotage implies taking actions against yourself, such as stopping yourself from achieving goals and driving away relationships (Jacobson, 2016). We do this by convincing ourselves that we don't truly want or need those things. Self-sabotage may sometimes look like impulsivity and a need for excitement in that you make a sudden decision that takes you away from something you had already planned. It can also take the form of indecision, like not wanting something that you wanted before when it starts to happen. Moreover, it can also take the form of self-criticism if you're making statements of low self-worth to convince yourself not to do the things you want. It can also appear as procrastination, defensiveness, and perfectionism when you're not doing something you want because you fear that you won't be able to achieve a perfect result.

Self-sabotage is very powerful because it can become a pattern: one act of self-sabotage will lead to another and become a programmed mechanism to suppress its trigger. With that said, we often self-sabotage because of the limiting beliefs and insecurities that surface when we're approaching the things we desire. So, we're left with two options: we can either take the easier road of staying in our comfort zone while continuing to stand in our own way or uncover and face these unconscious and negative thoughts, beliefs, and emotions in order to move forward. Self-sabotage often begins during childhood, in the form of defeating thoughts and behaviors that result from core traumas linked to feelings of inadequacy and internalizing misconceptions about ourselves. Furthermore, it is common to have internalized the things learned by our environment within our unconscious.

Another way we attempt to deal with trauma is by developing low self-worth. This is not, of course, something we consciously aim for; as per all protection mechanisms, it is developed as a means of coping. Low self-worth can result from an ongoing, deeply instilled belief that we are not as good as others. This thought pattern is irrational – an abundance of highly successful people think they are not enough. This often stems from unresolved past experiences and emotions that lead to negative beliefs about the world. Shame and being ashamed of who we are and what we've experienced is what drives low self-worth. Experiences that create shame and low self-worth include:

- Childhood abuse, where the person believes that it was their fault;
- Childhood traumas such as the loss of a loved one, neglect, bullying, or things that can affect the child's sense of self and safety;
- Poor parenting occurrences like unfair punishments, criticism, harsh standards, and lack of affection;
- Negative core beliefs including feeling less than, believing you're unlovable or feeling like something is wrong with you.

Low self-worth can lead to difficulties in relationships, defensiveness, blaming others, lack of boundaries, and victim mentality, among other things.

That said, self-sabotage and low self-worth are directly linked with negative thinking. That is because negative thinking leads to negative emotions and negative life choices (Jacobson, 2015). The signs that you're struggling with negative thinking are:

- Difficulty reaching your goals.
- Stopping yourself from doing the things you want to do.
- Constantly struggling in life.
- Believing the world is dangerous.
- Believing everyone else is happier than you.
- Thinking negatively of most people you're involved with.
- Being a pessimist.
- Having issues with most coworkers and family members.
- Sabotaging success.
- Constantly feeling stressed and anxious.

Negative thinking occurs when our thoughts try to convince us of something without any evidence. It can be a result of childhood trauma which might have happened for many reasons, including:

- Seeing our caregivers focus on the negative of the world, themselves, or others, to the point where it becomes a habit in us, and we don't question it.
- Childhood trauma which generally makes us see the world as dangerous and believe that we aren't safe or that we shouldn't trust anyone.
- Being criticized or shamed during childhood, which makes us internalize this negativity.

The Basics of The Work

In her book Loving What Is (2003), Byron Katie outlines her approach, which suggests that negative feelings are caused by our thoughts, either conscious or unconscious. Simply put, investigating the thought patterns behind our emotions is key to understanding them and working with them. Moreover, we tend to take our thoughts for granted or don't question their validity, which creates our suffering. In other words, we are attaching our emotional responses to our thoughts without filtering through the junk - without listening to our inner self. Thus, emotional pain becomes an inevitable part of our lives. Her approach, called "The Work," aims to develop our self-awareness. It does not rid our beings of thoughts and feelings but instead allows us to tidy the clutter of incessant thought flow. Ultimately, this leads to living a happy, fulfilling life full of love for ourselves and others, no matter our circumstances.

Byron Katie encourages us to use whatever is already within us and work with it. The approach is fairly simple: we have to question our thoughts and beliefs and then turn them around. When we're working with a thought or belief, the first question to ask ourselves is "is it true?". If the answer is 'yes,' then the second, "Can I absolutely know that it's true?", invites us to question ourselves more deeply. This is where we usually come face to face with self-limiting beliefs or distorted perceptions of reality. It leads us to the third question, which is "How do I react when I think that thought?" which helps us observe ourselves and our behaviors as reactions to our thoughts. This question is also of great importance when going through the shadow work process. It allows us to detect our triggers and dig deeper. Then, the fourth question, "Who would I be without that thought?" aims to get us to realize our potential beyond the constructed beliefs we have built within our psyche. This last question takes us out of our personal experience of the situation and allows us to view it from a non-egoic point of view. It leads us to witness how much harm our thinking patterns can cause us and to question our self-limiting beliefs. Answering honestly to these questions will lead to the Turnaround, which basically has to do with writing the opposite of our thoughts or beliefs. This helps us see the alternatives to our thoughts that might be true or truer than the original statement. This is the main idea of The Work, but we'll talk about it in more detail below.

Basic Principles

The first principle is about noticing how our thoughts argue with reality.

Reality is what it is and can't be changed. We can't change reality, only the way we perceive it. We can only accept it. As such, our suffering is caused by resisting what is, by expecting and wanting reality to be different. Nevertheless, accepting reality doesn't mean condoning it. It only means that we see things as they are and try to move forward. For example, if a person lost their job, they might be thinking about how unfair this was and that it shouldn't have happened. No matter why this happened, thinking this way won't change reality. There are many reasons to worry when experiencing a setback; however, it is up to us to change the situation or accept it as it is. Finding peace within what is (acceptance) and deciding what to do next will have the most positive impact on our well-being. Mindset is everything. Knowing how to stop overthinking what was and what might come to be will help us tap into our inner space and find the answers we are seeking.

The second principle is about staying in our own business.

There are three types of 'businesses': ours, other people's, and God's (meaning reality). Everything that is out of our or other people's control is the universe's business. B.K. argues that most of our suffering comes from living out of our own business. This means that when we attempt to judge or control what is beyond our control, we experience separation from our own lives. Furthermore, living in our own business (minding our own thoughts rather than personalizing or attempting to interpret others' perceptions) enables us to feel free.

The third principle is about meeting our thoughts with understanding.

Thoughts are harmless when we don't believe them. What causes harm is attachment to our thoughts, which means that we believe them and feed them without questioning them. In that, beliefs are thoughts we've been attaching to over the years. So, unquestioned thoughts become unquestioned beliefs that we live by without questioning their validity. Moreover, trying to stop our thoughts isn't possible. However, what is possible is to observe them, consider their validity, and release them.

The fourth principle is about becoming aware of our stories.

Stories about the past, the present, or the future are thoughts or sequences of thoughts that we believe are real. We tell ourselves stories many times a day about the events we lack information about. For instance, when someone walks out of the room abruptly, we might tell ourselves that

this person is angry or upset. This is an untested and uninves-
tigated theory to explain what is happening without us realizing that they are just theories. Judging and labeling (often
by giving credit to our thoughts) is a protection mechanism
that creates a sense of security. As for the theories our minds
create, they tend to snowball into all sorts of unpleasant situations and emotions. These can grow exponentially throughout
our existence; by extension, short stories breed bigger ones,
and these bigger stories breed major theories about our lives.
The Work's goal is to test the validity of these theories and
help us leave them aside while embracing the truth.

Lastly, the fifth principle underlies all aspects mentioned
above: Identifying the thoughts behind the creation of our
suffering.

As I said before, behind negative feelings are thoughts
that are rarely true, upon which we act and build our own
stories. This means that we try to change our feelings by
looking outside ourselves instead of understanding the original cause, which is the thought that our own mind has
shaped. In addition, we are usually aware of the feeling
before becoming conscious of the thought, meaning that the
feeling can alarm us or let us know that there is a thought we
need to work on. Putting our thoughts or stories against the
four questions helps us challenge them, which is the way into
inner peace.

The Work reminds us that all answers can be found within
us. It also aims at bringing out innate aspects of ourselves,
and after some time, this process becomes automatic. This
process is a precious pathway into observing and healing
ourselves, thus learning to tap into and embrace our shadow.

How to Do the Work

For the sake of simplicity, this is a quick overview of how to begin *The Work* for the purpose of encountering one's shadow.

The first step consists of pinpointing and writing down judgments you have formed about what is bothering you at the moment, for example, a stressful situation or a person who irritates you in your life. You may want to write about your mother, father, spouse, children, siblings, friends, acquaintances, boss, teacher, employee, coworker, and authority figures. However, it must be a specific incident or issue. After becoming accustomed to this, you can move on by writing about issues like money, health, body image, etc. As you gain experience with this process, you can begin to write about any uncomfortable thoughts you might have. It is important that you write down your thoughts without censoring them. Write spontaneously, without judgment, allowing yourself to release thoughts precisely as they are. This will help you understand your thoughts and behaviors and learn about repeating certain behavioral patterns.

The second step will be to use each of the four questions on each statement you've written. This will lead you to reflect on, if not uncover, the truth behind your perceptions. It will help you perceive any harmful ways of thinking. It is also a way to observe how you treat yourself in each situation.

The third step will be to turn it around. Therefore, find the opposite of your original assertion. This will help you find out what is true or truer in each situation. In other words, the turnarounds can provide answers to many of your struggles.

So, to conclude, you've now learned the foundational principles of The Work and how to begin this process. Practicing this method will lead you to be free from your thoughts and emotions yet much more deeply connected to yourself. If you start doing it, it will help you immensely in your journey inwards, facilitating the process of Shadow Work. In short, it's an excellent way to get to know the thoughts, beliefs, and feelings that reside in your Shadow and, ultimately, face your traumas.

There is an abundance of information available online, as well as Katie Byron's collection of work. You can find the relevant worksheets by clicking this link or visiting thework.com.

*D*oing The Work on yourself can be difficult, as it is quite challenging to remove ourselves from a personal situation already tainted with judgments and personal beliefs. If you have access to a person you trust, you may choose to have them assist you through the motions to facilitate this process.

No matter your choice throughout this journey, please allow your truth to be revealed. Let it flow from yourself unaltered so that you may see what is and begin to love yourself as you are.

4

OWNING YOUR DARKNESS

AVOIDING YOUR TRIGGERS ISN'T HEALING.

> *Healing happens when you're triggered and you're able to move through the pain, the pattern, and the story – and walk your way to a different ending.*

— Vienna Pharaon

*I*n Chapter 2, we discussed self-awareness and a few tips to get to know your personality. In this chapter, we will talk more about self-awareness and discuss more ways to achieve it. Self-awareness has to do with how you perceive, describe, and evaluate yourself in relation to others (Jacobson, 2019b). Your sense of self includes your qualities, defining characteristics, and responsibilities you think you have. It is heavily influenced by the environment in which we grew up. It is formed during childhood from imitating others until we find what works for us. When our sense of self is deficient, we experience an identity crisis because we can't cope. Having a poor sense of self and lack of self-awareness causes problems in our relationships; when we cannot understand ourselves, how can we expect others to understand us? Or we might be trying to find our identity through others, meaning that we might end up in unhealthy relationships or dependent on our partners. A poor sense of self usually stems from childhood trauma or emotional neglect. Not having someone to rely on and accept you during childhood can create this type of trauma, making you adapt to situations in order to receive love.

But before we talk about ways to develop self-awareness, we have to speak about complexes, as they are part of the Shadow. The notion of complexes is a concept that fascinated Jung, yet was first proposed by Freud. Complexes can be defined as core patterns of emotions, memories, or wishes revolving around a common theme, such as power or status (Schultz & Schultz, 2017). Furthermore, they unconsciously influence our thoughts, behaviors, and feelings and should be integrated to complete the process of individuation. Complexes reside in the unconscious, are related to trauma, and exceed our intentions. They can create conflicts, compulsive thoughts, and fuel actions. They are autonomous, meaning that they act without our conscious approval; unaware of the extent of their influence on our lives, we seldom know about them and have limited control over them.

A complex is created by a trauma (emotional shock) that splits a part of the psyche. This means that it creates an autonomous "splinter psyche" inside the personality while also being unconscious. This trauma makes the person behave in a way that overcompensates for what they're feeling. To illustrate, suppose that a child is constantly compared with a sibling, has a physical or mental condition, or is being treated unfavorably by their peers. This can create the trauma of not being good enough and unveil feelings associated with it, like sadness, shame, or jealousy. This might also bring on an Inferiority Complex. Now, to compensate for feeling inadequate, this person might put down others, insulting or belittling them (projection) to make themselves feel bigger or better. They might seek attention or be overly aggressive to compensate for their self-perceived 'inadequacies.' In addition, a complex is generally repressed, making it difficult to integrate as it creates conflicts in the psyche. Furthermore, according to this theory, at the core of any complex is an archetype (universal pattern of experience), like the Mother, the Hero, the Sovereign, etc., which is called an "Archetypal Alliance." The purpose of the Archetypal Alliance is to strengthen the complex so as to better defend and protect us (Zimberoff, 2017).

Complexes can appear in everyday life as slips of the tongue, personifications in dreams, or personal beliefs (West, n.d.). Surprisingly enough, complexes can be either good or bad, depending on whether they produce positive or negative results. So, integrating our complexes, though a challenging task because of the 'negative' qualities and traumas that might reside in them, is very helpful in the individuation process. It also happens to be an integral component of Shadow Work. Complexes function similarly to the Shadow because they are composed of 'unacceptable' parts of ourselves (like anger or sexuality) and traumas (like rejection or abuse). These aspects are interlinked. Another reason they are difficult to integrate is because fear and resistance are their main characteristics. Therefore, working with our anger, shame, and resistance are key factors to integrating complexes.

Just like the Shadow, **we develop beliefs and attitudes that support or reinforce our complexes towards others who embody the values of our complexes**.

We do this because it is easier to judge or blame others than to observe our own flaws. Therefore, it is vital to notice not only what bothers us in others but also our own behaviors that relate to what we do to avoid being like these other people that trigger us or to compensate for our negative feelings.

Moreover, when we see others embodying our complex, we feel that their behavior is unacceptable and unbearable. This triggered response is a huge Shadow Work red light; stop, observe how you feel, and ask yourself *why* you feel this way. When we begin to observe this process, we catch ourselves being triggered and re-traumatized. Sometimes these behaviors associated with our traumas are so internalized that we end up projecting them onto others, which creates all kinds of conflicts. It can create a cycle of shame and guilt, which is why healing from these wounds through encountering the Shadow is so important.

Meditation

Meditation is known as the skill of paying attention to your thoughts, your physical sensations or your body, and your emotions. There are numerous ways of meditating, and most of us prefer a different way, according to our needs. Here we'll talk about how to start meditating and, after you've gained some experience, how to find which method best suits you. The whole point of meditation is to help you notice what's happening inside and outside of you. With meditation, you're present and aware. It also helps with noticing your behavior, which is important because many of our behaviors are unconscious. This means that we think we know the motives behind our behaviors, but in reality, we don't. In fact, it is primarily unpleasant feelings that drive our impulsive behaviors. Therefore, meditation is an essential part of getting to know our Shadow.

Apart from self-awareness, meditation also improves our ability to regulate our emotions. It promotes self-control, empathy, patience, compassion, creativity and elevates our mood. Before you begin meditation or Shadow Work, try to center yourself. Even if you are working towards finding a calm, clear, and neutral state, you must do what you can (using breathwork, for instance) to ground and find your center. If you find yourself in a hyper-aroused state or distress, be kind to yourself by allowing emotions to flow out.

Begin your meditation with a compassionate mindset towards yourself. This means that you must find the strength to replace shame and guilt with friendliness, self-acceptance, and self-compassion. Allow yourself to keep an open mind so that you can accept the emotions, thoughts, and behaviors that will emerge, just as they are.

Having a Shadow is part of being human. Accept your humanness. If you don't enter the process with an open mind, you'll reject everything that will come out, which will hinder your progress. Remember, you have nothing to fear. It's just you and yourself. No one is there to judge, blame, or reject you. So, don't take the place of others by rejecting or judging yourself, as you don't need to step into anyone else's shoes. *Just allow yourself to be.* Accepting what is and working with it will help you release emotional pain and feel whole. Don't forget the big picture and your goal.

Find beauty in this process. Find beauty within your darkness.

Hold tight, breathe, and stay with me.

*R*esistance

Perhaps you've been putting off meditating for a while - heck, I avoided it for a very long time. Despite the benefits of meditation, many of us often resist or avoid this practice. This can generally be attributed to five major reasons, which are listed below. Consider these if necessary, as they do not apply to every individual.

1. Laziness. You might think that meditation is a tedious, passive process of just sitting there. However, I would argue that it's an active process that requires both mental and physical energy. Meditating in the morning is an excellent way to combat this obstacle, simply because we have more mental energy earlier in the day.

2. Achieving. Contrary to laziness, one might think that meditation is just a waste of time or that they are too busy to pause and practice meditation. On the other hand, due to this constant need to be reaching a goal, one might push themselves to meditate in a forced mental state for longer than they should, which won't produce any positive results.

3. Being ego-driven. Some might choose to meditate because it is 'cool' or because many people do it nowadays. It can also become part of their identity and lead to ego inflation (believing you're better

than others because you meditate). This happens due to the need for belonging and self-esteem. In other words, these people want to belong to the group of 'enlightened' people who meditate and, because of that, persuade themselves of being superior to others. These unconscious motivations lead to resistance in cultivating a meaningful practice.

4. Unconscious shame. Tied to the previous notion of being ego-driven, unconscious shame derives from being told that you 'should' meditate or that meditation somehow makes you morally superior. Acknowledging this shame will help you build a better practice.

5. Unconscious hatred or feeling obligated. Some people who meditate (even meditation instructors) dislike the process, inadvertently transferring this sentiment onto their students. The instructor might be unconscious of this hatred and transmit their own feelings of resistance to others.

*P*sychological Benefits

Meditation is key in developing self-awareness as it will enable you to become an observer of your thoughts. Being the observer is associated with the Magician archetype, which means that it will also help you solidify a Quarter of your Container. In other words, observing creates a space between you (the experiencer) and the observer self. This space will help you identify some unconscious emotions, thoughts, and behaviors. It also helps in the process of individuation by opening up the unconscious. Meditation can put you in a trance-like state where you are more centered, calm, and open. When dealing with anything that has to do with the unconscious, Shadow Work included, you need to be in that kind of state so that you don't criticize or reject whatever comes up.

Nevertheless, this does not mean that you should just accept anything during meditation without questioning it. It only means that you are more prone to perceiving and accepting something that you would otherwise reject if you weren't in a meditative state. Thus, meditation keeps you centered when dealing with repressed traits or emotions and is, therefore, a very powerful tool for Shadow Work.

How to Start Off

Knowing that meditation is beneficial for your mind and body is the first step to practicing it. Nevertheless, without guidance, most people are left wondering what to do and how to meditate. Therefore, a simple way to begin is by focusing your attention on something specific. This can be an object, your breath, a body part, a sound, or a thought. What is important here is that you maintain your attention to it. For example, if you choose to focus on your breath, notice how you breathe - observe how you inhale and exhale. You might get distracted, in which case you can kindly remind yourself to redirect your observation to your breath. Try to observe how it feels to breathe. You can do this by observing the sensation in your nose or lungs. Start by doing this for one or two minutes at a time, however long feels comfortable, until you begin to ease into this ritual.

Another way to meditate is called grounding. This means

that you observe how you are fully present in your body and connected to the earth (Jeffrey, 2017c). When you're ungrounded, it is common to get distracted easily, overthink, engage in drama, experience anxiety and worry, desire material things, be easily deceived, and be obsessed with your external appearance. To move away from these hindering thought patterns, you can start this practice by reconnecting with your body.

There are many exercises for grounding, a few of which I have listed below:

- Feel your feet. Place all your awareness and feel the sensations at the bottom of your feet. You can do this while sitting or standing, and it takes about one minute.

- Follow your breath as you inhale and exhale. Feel the air entering and leaving your lungs and nose. This takes about 10 minutes.

- Stand like a tree. For about 10 minutes, stand with your feet parallel and shoulder-width apart. Tuck your chin and keep your spine straight while resting your hands at your side. Feel your body's tension sinking into your feet and allow it to be absorbed from the ground.

Feel free to explore meditative practices as you please.

You will find an abundance of practical tools and tips in *The Well-Being Handbook: A complete guide to optimal wellness, positive habits & holistic self-care.* There is no right or wrong way to go about this; choose the most sustainable path, the one that feels right for you.

Identifying Your Personal Values

The identification of personal values is central to the discussion of self-awareness. By clarifying your values, you'll start making more meaningful choices that are in accordance with your most authentic self. Consequently, you'll be able to make decisions faster, your thinking will be clearer, you will choose friends and partners who suit you, you'll be at peace with yourself, your life purpose will be clearer, and your self-esteem will be higher. In some cases, we end up with an unfavorable set of values because, as children, we weren't encouraged to be ourselves. Perhaps you were raised with one of these patterns:

- You received love and affection only if you were 'good' (pleasing your primary caregiver).
- You didn't develop a safe and secure attachment to your caregiver.
- You received unfair punishment for typical behaviors, and you learned to be invisible.
- Your parents were very successful and dominant and raised you to be like them.
- You had a big, crowded family, which made you learn to adapt to your environment in order to protect yourself.
- You experienced emotional, physical, or sexual abuse that taught you to repress and avoid speaking your mind.

These experiences might have caused you to rely on others to know what's right, to lack boundaries, and to rely on the opinions of others to establish what is best for you.

In this case, you will need to dig deeper to find out if your values are, in truth, your own. To do this, you can ask yourself the following questions:

1. Think about the last three big decisions you made. Did they make you feel energized or tired/overwhelmed?
2. When you are speaking, do you feel excited and inspired, or do you feel like you're listening to someone else?
3. Write down your top values and read them aloud. How do these make you feel? Are you at peace with these or slightly uncomfortable?
4. If you had a week left to live and wrote down a schedule, would it match the five values you wrote about earlier?
5. Look again at the five values you wrote. Who in your environment encompasses these values? Can you see who or where you learned them from? Why did you choose these, specifically? Are they supporting your personal journey and self-fulfillment?

Core values underlie our entire existence, encompassing our thoughts and guiding our life force. Common personal values are loyalty, respect, honesty, fidelity, kindness, compassion, and integrity (the list goes on). Now, the first step to getting to know your true values is to start with the mind of a beginner (Jeffrey, 2014b). This means that you don't have preconceived ideas of what they should be. In other words, consider your answers in the above list. If you've realized that some of your values (if not all of them) might not truly be your own, it's time to put them aside and start exploring your authentic self. Ah, yes, digging deeper is the journey we are taking throughout this book: uncovering your core values - ones that might have been repressed for some time - and revealing your true being.

To help tap into your values, you can do the following:

1. Think about the happiest time of your life. What about this memory made you so happy? Can you see a personal value in it?
2. Write down the things you've done and are most proud of, regardless of what others thought. What values do they show?

The second step is to consider the suppressed values (the true ones) you might have. You can answer the following to uncover them:

1. If you won the lottery, what would you do with your life? Write down what your life would look like with no financial issues. Then, consider what values this plan reflects.
2. Write down three characters you admire (fictional, personal acquaintances, celebrities, etc.). What is it that you admire in them? What values do you share or would like to share with this person?
3. Think about a time you got angry, frustrated, or upset. Then, turn the situation around and think about what values might have been suppressed at that point in time.

The third step is to write down a list of values you have

and group them into related themes. For example, learning, growth, and development are related.

Then, the fourth step is to highlight the central theme of each value. In the previous example, all three words can be summarized under the category of growth. For the next step, consider the following:

1. Which of these values are essential to your well-being, lifestyle, and peace of mind?
2. Which of them best represents you and the way you would like to be? For example, if I am striving to be a kind person, the category of empathy, which includes compassion, respect, and understanding, is the category I would value the most.
3. Which of these values are essential to supporting your personal growth and happiness?

Now, have a look at the values you're left with. Most people have between five and ten core values, but there is no right or wrong answer here. Rank these values according to their importance, for example, 1 being the most important and 5 being the least important.

After discovering your true personal values, you need to reflect on the way in which you are currently living by these. To begin thinking about this, you can use the list of your values. Rate each value from 1 to 10 according to how much you believe you are living in accordance with it, with 1 representing not living with this value at all and 10 representing fully encompassing this value from day to day. For a rating below 7, think about what changes you could make in order to live according to this value. Keep revisiting the list each month. This is especially important when you're making important decisions to determine if your current choices still align with your core values.

Starting Shadow Work

At this point, simply by navigating and reflecting on the content we've discussed so far, you've already made considerable progress on your Shadow Work journey. Now that you've thought about and pinpointed some elements of your Shadow, you'll want to try to contextualize them. Here's an easy exercise to help you do this (Lavers, 2020):

1. Write a list of things that trigger or annoy you in others. Use what you've learned in the previous chapters to identify these.
2. Choose one to focus on. After you've worked on one quality, you can move on to the next.
3. Imagine a person expressing this quality (behavior).
4. Pay attention to your body. Are you feeling your face pulling an expression? Tension in your neck? Which emotions try to surface? What sensations run through your body? For maximum results, do this during meditation.
5. As you get deeper into a meditative state, distance yourself from your physical presence. Allow your observer self to witness the situation without getting emotionally involved.
6. Without judgment, accept the emotions that are surfacing. Accepting your emotions is key to accepting yourself.

7. Now you can let the image go. Release the thought. Release the feelings.

8. Repeat to yourself, "I am everything. I am (quality)".

9. Repeat steps 4, 5, and 6.

10. Repeat to yourself several positive qualities you have as well as the quality you're focusing on. For example, you can say, "I am everything. I am generous.", and then "I am everything. I am jealous.". This step is key to unlocking self-forgiveness and acceptance of oneself.

11. Notice how much more tolerable this quality feels now.

12. Sit with the results and think about them at a later time or, perhaps, at another session of meditation.

Gaining Perspective

In the previous chapter, we talked about how the Sovereign energy is the second Quarter of your Container. It is now time to start building that. So, after you've tried the exercise above and have identified what upsets or triggers you in others, you can now put it into context. The first step is to **notice**. Try to recall the specific situation in which someone else's behavior annoyed you. Notice and **experience** the emotions you were feeling at that time, and try to find the reason you were upset.

The next step is to **write**. This helps you record your thoughts and feelings in order to become aware of your unconscious (Centre of Excellence, 2019) and gain clarity. Use simple sentences to talk about the following:

1. What do you want this person to change, and what do you want them to do?
2. What advice would you give this person?
3. What would you want this person to tell you, do, think, or feel in order for you to feel happy?
4. What are your thoughts of this person in this situation?
5. What about this situation would you never want to experience again?

The third step is to **question** what you just wrote. Go back to each statement and ask the following questions about it. Do this for all your answers to the above questions.

1. Is it true? (reply with just yes or no)
2. Can you absolutely know that it's true? (reply with just yes or no)
3. How do you react, and what happens when you believe that thought?
4. Who would you be without that thought?

Now, as Byron Katie would say, it's time to Turn It Around. You will now turn it around and find the opposites of your statements.

1. Find the opposites. For instance, if your statement is "Jasper doesn't listen to me," you can turn it around as "I don't listen to myself," "I don't listen to Jasper," or "Jasper listens to me."
2. Turn around to your thinking. This means that you should turn around what you want from your outer self to your inner self. For example, if you say, "I

want my body to be healthy and strong," turn it around to "I want my thinking to be healthy and strong."

3. Turn around to Statement 5. If your original thought was, "I don't want Jasper to lie to me ever again," turn it around to "I am willing/looking forward to Jasper lying to me again."

4. Find examples. Think about how each turnaround is truer than the original statement. You need to find at least three examples of how each turnaround is true. This will help you find alternatives.

5. Avoid turning around the turnaround. This means that you should think critically before deciding which turnarounds are valid. For instance, the turnarounds "I shouldn't listen to myself" or "I shouldn't listen to Jasper" are not valid.

(Byron Katie, n.d.)

*N*ow that you've learned about meditation, applying foundational concepts of *The Work*, and how to start off with Shadow Work, it is time to keep exploring by learning to recognize the specific qualities that are your Shadow.

In the next chapter, we will talk about how projection works, the different forms it can take, and how to stop it before it damages your relationships. As we continue our journey, you will also learn how to rebuild your emotional body.

5

BEING FEARLESS

When you finally learn that a person's behavior has more to do with their own internal struggles than you, you learn grace.

— ALLISON AARS

*I*n this chapter, we will talk about an important defense mechanism that is often well embedded within the psyche: Projection. As a starting point for Shadow Work, you will discover how this unconscious mechanism intended to protect you can keep you from tapping into your most authentic self. You'll also learn how to cope with the darkness within and equip yourself with some tools you might need in order to face your traumas.

Projection

As I've said before, projection is when we transfer our unacceptable traits and impulses onto others. We do this without realizing we're doing it to avoid facing these unconscious traits or impulses that are held within us. As such, projection is considered a defense mechanism since it protects us from facing something that will be painful (Vinney, 2021). It is important to remember that we don't consciously decide to project; we do this automatically to protect our egos. All defense mechanisms are instinctive, meaning that we don't consciously choose to use them. They emerge on their own when we are in danger, either real or perceived. That is why we don't usually recognize that we are projecting unless we've learned how to detect our triggers and defensive reactions. Most of us constantly project our opinions, fears, and insecurities onto others (like telling someone they should or shouldn't do a particular thing) because we have this idea or belief that it is wrong/dangerous/inappropriate/etc.

In that matter, defense mechanisms are unconscious strategies that we use to defend the ego against psychic dangers or characteristics that would cause conflict or anxiety in the psyche. Projection is usually used after mid-childhood because it is then that the child has fully developed their conscience. This means that it depends on our primitive understanding of right and wrong in a black and white sense. Projection is commonly used during childhood until we develop more mature defense mechanisms such as identification (internalizing and imitating another person's behavior). However, this doesn't mean that adults don't use it – on the contrary, it is used abundantly by individuals from all walks of life.

Now, here is a simple example of projection. A married woman secretly likes her male co-worker, but won't admit it, so she gets jealous of her husband when he talks with a female co-worker, believing that he likes her. Attributing our own beliefs and suppressed emotions to others is a common form of projection.

It has been found that people with low self-esteem who feel inferior and don't know themselves well are more prone to projecting (Lindberg, 2018). It is important to note here that seeing our positive or neutral characteristics in others is different because, in this case, we're not trying to protect our egos. We indeed tend to overestimate people who have similar characteristics to us, but this is called false consensus and isn't projection.

As I have said before, the psyche is always doing what's best for it, and defense mechanisms help it protect itself. However, projection is helpful in the short term, but not in the long term. It's like putting a bandage over a scratch and believing that it's not there because you can't see it. In this case, projection helps us maintain our illusion of self-esteem, but that's about it. It can be harmful in the long run because it disrupts our relationships with others and can lead to bullying, jealousy, distorted perceptions of reality, and victim-blaming.

Although defense mechanisms are unconscious, it is still possible to recognize our projections. Detecting triggers and intercepting these mechanisms is also an integral part of Shadow Work. If you're still struggling with pinpointing what irritates you, keep in mind that whatever feels uncomfortable or whichever thoughts and feelings you're trying to avoid should be revisited and considered as possible triggers. This means that they bring to the surface parts of your Shadow.

Try to be truthful to yourself about what makes you anxious or irritates you, and don't be afraid to dig deeper into traits you don't like about yourself. Keep in mind that you are alone in this process; no one can criticize you. The only person you are truly accountable to is yourself. It is crucial that you try to view your behavior as objectively as possible. Working on noticing when you inadvertently use this defense mechanism will help you foster self-awareness and elucidate parts of your shadow self.

The Darkness Within

Getting to know your Shadow requires you to ask yourself a few hard questions and really reflect on your answers. You don't need to analyze what you wrote down extensively. You can simply begin by asking yourself these questions, note your answers, and contemplate them at a later time. This step, however, is essential because answering these questions will help you reveal additional components of your Shadow. So, you can ask yourself the following, ideally when you're in a meditative state:

1. What do I most need to be forgiven for? This will reveal the situation for which you feel guilt or regret.
2. In what way would my life be different if I didn't feel this guilt, regret, or shame?
3. What would be available to me if I forgave myself?

It is important to note here that the Shadow isn't neces- sarily consistent. Values can be added or taken away from it, depending on what is happening in your life. The density and rigidity of the Shadow increases when you're doing the following (Chopra et al., 2011):

- Keeping secrets. Secrecy can result from denial, deliberate deception of others, fear of exposing your true self and having been conditioned by your family. This way, your Shadow accumulates material to build upon.

- Guilt and shame. People who feel guilt about their flaws and shame about their mistakes end up bottling up those emotions. This gives more power to the Shadow since it is mainly built on shame or guilt.

- Judgment. When you can't find a way to release bottled-up guilt and shame, you often use judgment to say that you or others deserve it in order to disguise your pain.

- Blame avoidance. This means that you blame others who you think are inferior because you believe that your suffering is a moral issue caused by them.

- Projection.

- *You vs. them* mentality. This means that you separate yourself from others to the point where you believe that only you are on the 'good' side. However, it can create isolation and increase fear or suspicion, which fuels the darker side of your Shadow.

- Keeping evil away. If you're convinced that evil is everywhere, then this will create a struggle, which will feed the Shadow.

Stopping Projection

The first step to combating these issues is to stop projecting. To do this, you'll need to start by identifying when you're projecting and determining the different forms projection can take. The different forms of projection are the following:

- Superiority. This means that you feel like you're better than others and demand that others see this and recognize it. Superiority comes from believing deep down that you're a failure and that others will reject you if they see who you actually are.

- Injustice. It has to do with believing that bad things are happening to you unfairly and that you don't deserve them. Moreover, it comes from the unconscious belief that you're sinful and that you're always to blame.

- Arrogance. This means that you're irritated by the presence of others, which stems from repressed anger and, beneath that, deep-rooted pain.

- Defensiveness. It is related to disregarding others when you're feeling that they're attacking you. It comes from the trauma of feeling unworthy and weak.

- Blaming others. Believing that your mistakes or actions are somebody else's fault disguising the deep trauma of you being to blame for everything and that you should be ashamed of yourself.

- Idealization. This means that you think of certain people as gods. This comes from unconsciously feeling like a weak and helpless child who depends on others for protection and care.

- Prejudice. Grouping together people with common characteristics is a natural tendency for humans. Namely, racism is an issue stemming from this kind of thinking, as well as the *Us vs. Them* mentality, among other factors. There's much debate about whether our brains just work like this or if we're taught to think in such a way as a result of our upbringing or social conditioning. However, grouping people with shared characteristics into one category (categorizing them) isn't a problem on its own. The problem is created when we ascribe to this category of people with negative traits. This is called prejudice and can be applied to many situations and include different factors like age, gender, race, occupation, social status, physical or mental health, etc. I'm sure you can see how this can be dangerous to society. In our case, prejudice might disguise the unconscious trauma of feeling like we're inferior and deserve to be rejected.

- Jealousy. This has to do with feeling like others (especially romantic partners) will betray you.

This suspicious attitude often stems from the deep-rooted belief of being inadequate (sexually) and may disguise our own impulse to betray our partner.

- Paranoia. This is the belief that others are out to get you or that there is a conspiracy only you can see. This mechanism soothes deep-seated, overwhelming anxiety related to not feeling safe.

*S*o, to recap, projection has to do with negative energy both on the inside and the outside. This means that it happens when you're feeling a negative emotion and aiming it at someone else or seeking other reasons to justify them. Nevertheless, it is necessary not to confuse negative emotions that are constructive with negative energy. For instance, being angry is a legitimate feeling, but blaming others for triggering our own anger isn't okay.

After you've identified your behaviors related to projection, you'll need to tap into your hidden feelings. This means that when you catch yourself feeling the hidden emotion, be it anger or shame or whichever comes to the surface, that is the right moment to pause and observe what is happening. That is, before your ego starts to defend itself. To do that, though, you'll need to be alert, open, honest, and willing. It will take courage to make peace with these emotions. However, if you don't do the work, you can be assured that they will persist and continue their harmful cycle within your Shadow self.

Simply put, what you need to do is acknowledge your feelings so that they stop being unwanted. You don't have to love or welcome them yet, but recognizing their existence is a considerable step in the right direction. Repetitively recognizing your emotions without judgment will begin to alter their form in thought, at once removing guilt and shame. You will soon begin to feel lighter in their presence, noticing them being expressed in a healthier way.

This is you, laying a solid foundation for lasting healing.

Detaching

Understandably, the process of letting go of negative emotions is a hard one. That is because these emotions hide others underneath them within the Shadow. After you have practiced acknowledging your emotions, you'll need to learn to detach yourself from negativity. This is a bit tricky because you'll want to take responsibility for your emotions (like "This anger is mine") but not completely identify with them (like "I am my anger"). People tend to attach themselves to their negative energy when it arises and act as if they can't let go. The following thought patterns demonstrate how we attach to and internalize our negative emotions:

- Thinking that you don't deserve what is happening to you and asking, "Why me?".
- Thinking that you aren't responsible for the situation and that somebody must pay for it.
- Wanting to vent on someone else.
- Feeling like the situation is making you crazy.
- Thinking that nobody can help you.

- Trying to find distractions in order to forget about the problem.
- Wanting to use substances to feel better.
- Wanting to be rescued.
- Thinking that somebody has it in for you.
- Wanting to settle the situation right now.
- Thinking that you can't do anything about how you're feeling.

So, to detach, turn these around. Namely, remind yourself that:

- It won't last forever, and you'll get through it.
- You can deal with the emotion since you've felt it before.
- Venting on someone else won't make you feel better.
- Acting out will lead to guilt and regret.
- If you wait for some time, you will cool down and make better decisions.
- You are not alone.
- You can talk to someone you trust.
- You are more than your feelings.
- You alone can alter your thoughts and emotions.
- Moods come and go.

Giving Up Self-Judgment

We all tend to judge our feelings as 'good' or 'bad.' All emotions are valid. At times, positive emotions can be harmful, while negative ones can be beneficial. However, it is self-judgment that truly causes damage. For example, someone who is trying to be helpful, a positive feeling, can become very intrusive and, thus, turn it into something damaging. Judging our emotions doesn't leave space for us to be our true selves. What we need to do instead is to look at them with empathy. We all have an internal judge, an inner voice who criticizes us harshly for our mistakes. If you start empathizing with yourself, this judge will start to dissolve. Letting go of your judgment will make your conscience less critical and self-destructive.

Below are 11 signs that you are overly self-critical (Blundell, 2019):

1. You have different standards for yourself than your friends. Think about the last time a friend of yours had a problem. Did you support them? Do you treat yourself the same way?

2. You deflect compliments. Highly self-critical people tend to make excuses for or diminish compliments. Not being able to just say "thank you" and accept the compliment disguises the unconscious belief that you are flawed and can never do or be enough.

3. People close to you are always criticizing you. This means that you might be seeing yourself as a victim of other people's criticism. In reality, we often choose these kinds of people because they mirror what we think.

4. You agree to go along with others but often come to regret it. This happens because we project onto others the need for approval that we aren't getting from ourselves.

5. You blame yourself when things go wrong. You might be doing this even in situations where the outcome isn't within your control.

6. Your parents were extremely critical. Maybe they criticized you for the way you behaved, made you feel like you weren't enough, or compared you with your sibling(s). Instead of criticizing you verbally, they might have done this by not giving you love or attention unless you were 'good.' This means that self-criticism is a learned behavior because we tend to internalize our parents' criticism into an internal (critical) voice.

7. You experienced a difficult/traumatic childhood. You might have been left with the idea that you aren't good enough because you couldn't stop bad things from happening.

8. You feel like you can't keep up with what needs to be done. Are you able to recognize your achievements or give yourself credit for your accomplishments?

9. You compare yourself to others. This becomes a habit, and it's a form of self-criticism.

10. You focus on what isn't working. Your thinking is black and white, meaning that you believe you're either a good or a bad person, depending on the day.

11. You feel like you are not succeeding in life, despite your efforts. This happens because of the vast amounts of energy self-criticism requires. Continually feeling unsuccessful can also stop us from taking chances and recognizing opportunities.

Self-judgment manifests as an inner critic, which is a form of projection directed towards the self. Our inner critic tends to reflect everything that is good in a negative way so that it looks horrible or unimportant (Stone & Stone, 1993). In some people, the inner critic is stronger than in others, but, ultimately, we all have one. This is an inner voice that speaks to us – about us - in a negative way. In fact, our inner critic has come to feel natural to us because we've all developed it since our childhoods by adopting our environment's judgments about our own person and society's expectations.

Now, unbelievable as it might seem, the inner critic's function is actually to protect us from being shamed and hurt. When we are children, it is common for our parents or caregivers to try to figure out our 'bad' traits and fix them to give us more opportunities for success in the world. This means that we receive from our parents the message that there is something wrong with us that needs to be fixed. Therefore, we try to protect ourselves from feeling inadequate by developing this voice that adopts our parents' concerns, and end up criticizing ourselves before anyone else can.

This subpersonality is anxious and desperate for us to succeed in the world and be accepted. Furthermore, the inner critic is aware at all times. Most of us can't recognize the inner critic because it is unconscious, but it manages to control our lives nevertheless. It is modeled after a protective yet critical parent and cannot be appeased. Some of its common statements are:

- "The problem with you is …"
- "Don't be selfish/mean/ugly, etc."
- "You shouldn't have said/done that."

The inner critic is mostly evident in statements including the modal verb 'should,' implying that we're always making mistakes and that mistakes are unacceptable. Our inner critic tends to hinder our personal growth and is the source of low self-esteem because it constantly reminds us of what is wrong with our thinking, doing, and being. It is also a source of shame because it reminds us that we're not good enough.

The inner critic's misdirected intentions can snowball into unhealthy thought patterns and leave us unable to act in our best interest. The 10 most common traits of the inner critic are:

1. It stops you from being creative.
2. It prevents you from taking risks due to fear of failure.
3. It sees all your mistakes, including those you've already made and those you'll make in the future.
4. It makes you feel inferior to others and compares you to them.
5. It warns you not to look foolish.
6. It monitors all your behaviors in order to avoid feeling shame.
7. It tells you that you're not good enough, lowering your self-esteem.
8. It has a negative view of your external appearance.
9. It doesn't allow you to recognize the positive feelings others have towards you.
10. It makes you susceptible to other people's judgments.

The inner critic mainly stems from fear of abandonment. This can surface due to parental neglect or rejection during childhood and sometimes even later in life (Jacobson, n.d.). Fear of abandonment makes us not let other people close to us (fear of intimacy) and make us seem cold, clingy, or controlling. People living with this fear of abandonment often believe that they can't trust others, that they are unlovable, that they don't deserve love, and that the world is a dangerous place. Moreover, they feel lonely with partners, making a point of leaving first if they believe that the other person will abandon them, are oversensitive and reactive, don't have good boundaries, and feel like they never fit in.

In short, people living with this deeply rooted trauma do everything in their power to prevent rejection or abandonment, either by being too clingy or by showing an emotionally cold face to the world. As such, the inner critic often emerges as a way of preventing the person from being abandoned once again, or rather, of reliving that trauma. In fact, it attempts to protect us in many different ways. Many subpersonalities work closely with the inner critic, which can develop depending on the environment we grew up in.

The Pleaser

The Pleaser is a type of inner critic that encourages us to do what others want so that we receive their love and approval. This way, it protects our vulnerability. It also suppresses and makes us disown parts of the self that don't please others. For example, a child notices that their mother is happier and gives more love to them when they're smiling. In this case, the Pleaser will tell the child to smile more and show less anger or unhappiness, to obtain validation from their caregiver. This also means that anger will become a disowned self and likely end up in the Shadow.

. . .

The Rule Maker

This subpersonality makes up the rules of who we should be and which of our traits are unacceptable. The rule maker develops early in life and protects us from vulnerability. It develops a set of rules according to what is rewarded and punished around us. Consequentially, the rule maker reinforces whatever is rewarded and whatever is punished is disowned and buried in the Shadow. In other words, the rule-maker sets the standards by which the inner critic tries to live. Like the inner critic, the rule maker is developed according to the expectations of our parents and society, and, in most cases, these standards are unattainable.

The Pusher

The pusher usually develops to help us perform in school and work since it is its job to get us to achieve our goals. It is never satisfied and always sets more goals for us because it wants us to gain recognition and succeed in the world. The pusher is overly ambitious and works well with the critic.

The Perfectionist

The perfectionist wants us to be, act, and look perfect. It wants to help us succeed in the world, like the pusher. It wants us to perform flawlessly in whatever we're doing, even if there is no need for perfection. For example, if you take on a hobby for fun, like drawing, and you're just doing it to enjoy yourself, the perfectionist wants you to become a great painter, even if no one will ever see your paintings. The perfectionists' standards for achievement can rarely be met.

Getting to Know Your Inner Critic

Becoming aware of the inner critic is the first step towards distancing yourself from it. The following are a few questions and exercises to help you get to know your inner critic.

Tune in to your inner critic. Notice and pay attention to the things you say to yourself or feel about yourself. The most important things to focus on are those that trigger negative emotions, which are often things you can't stand about yourself. Take note of the following:

1. What does your inner critic think is wrong with you?
2. What mistakes did you make during the day?
3. What is your critic telling you that you could have done better?
4. What do you feel you have overlooked?
5. What should you have done differently?

The things you note that create dissatisfaction with yourself are the judgments of your inner critic. Writing them down will help you reflect later and perhaps help you begin to alter your internal dialogues.

1. Find out what it looks like. On a piece of paper, draw your inner critic as you perceive it. In some way, this is a visual representation of a part of your Shadow. It could be a person you know, an animal, or anything else; it is yours, a part of you, for better or worse. You can also give it a name and personality. This might appear to be a silly exercise, but bringing your critic to life makes it easier to accept and tame it.

2. Then, use the statements of your inner critic (refer back to the first question) and answer the following questions, preferably in writing:

3. Does this sound like someone I know?

4. When did I first start being concerned about this issue? For example, when did I first start being concerned about being lazy?

5. Think of how your parents judged other people and write down some of their most frequent judgments about others.

6. Write down which traits a person could have that you deem unacceptable, according to your environment. Where did these originate? Are they a product of your upbringing or environment? Are these traits sometimes acceptable in other settings or environments? Are they acceptable in a different context and by other people? Take time to reflect on the underlying reasons for selecting these traits.

*R*ebuilding *Your Emotional Body*

By the term "emotional body," we refer to the bridge between the physical and the mental world. Suppressed emotions tend to emerge as discomfort, soreness, fatigue, or pain within the emotional body. So, rebuilding your emotional body will necessitate replacing negative emotions with something new. You can heal your emotional body by tapping into your authentic self.

By learning resilience, letting go of demons from your past, healing past trauma, expecting good things for yourself, adapting your ideals to become more realistic, being generous and compassionate, seeing through your fear, accepting yourself as you are, and communicating with your higher self, you will unleash your full potential and embody the truest version of yourself.

∼

*O*ver the last few pages, we've learned about projection and how to stop it, as well as how to detach ourselves from our thoughts, give up self-judgment, and rebuild our emotional body.

In Chapter 6, we'll talk about healing – our driving force in navigating our Shadow. There, you'll learn strategies to accept and release your traumas. We will explore Inner Child healing, and I will offer you some journaling prompts for Inner Child Work and Shadow Work.

6

HEALING

 The place where light and dark begin to touch is where miracles arise.

— Robert A. Johnson

Since most physical, psychological, and mental traumas happen during childhood, most of us don't remember them. We make decisions to protect ourselves when something that we can't control is happening, as seen previously through the exploration of defense mechanisms and unconscious triggers. These decisions were the best we could make at that time and were based on a child's understanding, which means that they may not have been the most beneficial. As adults, there are different ways in which our traumas can manifest. I guess we could call these psychosomatic repercussions, namely:

- Feeling like you're choking when you're speaking up.
- Pain in your stomach in certain situations.
- Tight or painful shoulders, as if you're carrying something heavy.
- Pain in the genital area during sex.
- Pain in your feet when your boundaries are being overstepped, and you don't speak up.

As you can see, these are physical repercussions of suppressed traumas. Considering that traumas throughout the spectrum give rise to intense emotions and pain, we tend to repress them in order to not feel or deal with these unpleasant feelings. This is an emotional regulation strategy, and it helps protect our psyche.

Nevertheless, when we bury these emotions, they still exist, and we end up carrying them with us throughout our lives. This creates stagnated energy, which in turn manifests as the physical symptoms we will talk about in the following pages. The wounds trauma leaves behind can also create triggers, which leaves us re-living these traumatic experiences.

These wounds prevent us from seizing opportunities, creating fulfilling relationships, and feeling connected to ourselves and others. Ultimately, in many ways, unresolved trauma will keep us from reaching our full potential.

Accepting and Releasing Trauma

The first step to healing from your trauma is to accept it. As in dealing with your Shadow, you must acknowledge that it is a part of you.

After that, you'll need to start paying attention to your

emotions and the situations which trigger your alarm responses or intense negative feelings. We've explored this previously when discussing defense mechanisms and the inner critic. If you can uncover your trigger, you can begin to identify your trauma. Now, this is by no means an easy task: It has been found that the brain's ability to form or maintain memories is impacted by trauma, meaning that we don't always remember our traumatic experiences. Moreover, as we've also seen, not remembering traumatic events can also be attributed to repression as a way to cope with the impact of the trauma.

Here are some signs that you may have repressed trauma:

1. Strong reactions to specific people or situations that can't be explained. Feeling 'off' about someone or a situation may mean that your brain is trying to warn you that you're not safe. As a reaction, your body might take a defensive position, or you might want to escape the situation. This can mean that this person reminds you of someone else who traumatized you or that the situation you're in right now is similar to the traumatic event of the past.

2. Extreme emotional shifts. For people with repressed trauma, emotion regulation is much more difficult. This means that you might go from being at ease to being extremely scared or angry for seemingly no reason. This would also indicate that even small, everyday things are linked to the repressed trauma.

3. Attachment issues. There are various types of attachment disorders, such as having an intense

fear of abandonment. The type and intensity will usually vary according to the nature of the trauma.

4. Anxiety. Those with repressed trauma generally experience more anxiety than others.

5. Childish reactions. Immaturity and outbursts are typical in cases of repressed trauma. These include throwing tantrums, speaking in a childlike voice or manner, or being stubborn about small things. Childlike behaviors are common in people with repressed trauma.

6. Chronic exhaustion. This comes from the energy required to keep these memories repressed, as well as going about our lives carrying the physical, mental and emotional repercussions of trauma.

7. Inability to cope with stress. This refers to typical stressful situations in which people with repressed trauma tend to feel unable to cope.

Childhood trauma usually emerges when we overreact in situations without really knowing why. For example, if someone tells you that they don't like what you're wearing today and you get extremely angry, sad, or ashamed, then you might have a trauma related to your external appearance. Perhaps you were put down or bullied as a child for your appearance, lack of hygiene, or worn-out wardrobe. With that said, emotional scars can have long-lasting effects that we have to live with. For instance, traumas are the reason some people are afraid to speak up when treated unfairly or why we have certain insecurities. Traumas are related to shame and guilt, and, as we know, these are the core emotions of the Shadow.

Some events that can cause trauma are:

- Physical, emotional, and sexual abuse.
- Violence in the school or community.
- Death or loss of someone close to us.
- Domestic violence, disasters, or terrorism (witnessing or experiencing it ourselves).
- Immigration or war.
- Neglect.
- Accidents.
- Life-threatening illnesses.

Moreover, trauma works like grief. That is because when you get emotionally injured, it feels like you've lost something in you, for which you now need to grieve. As most of us know, there are five stages in the grieving process, which also apply to trauma:

1. Denial - not believing that this is happening or has happened to you.
2. Anger - being angry because you don't understand the reason this happened.
3. Bargaining - contemplating what you or someone should have done differently or what could be done to change the course of events.
4. Depression - feelings of emptiness and that there's no point in anything due to having to face very intense emotions and adapt to them quickly.
5. Acceptance.

The goal for healing trauma is to reach acceptance and then try to resolve the emotions, thoughts, and behaviors associated with it. This is where Shadow Work comes into play, offering tools and techniques for healing.

Extracting the Trauma

This technique has to do with the embodied metaphor. Expressions like "having a burden on your shoulders" or "not being able to take your feet off the ground" use the body as a metaphor to describe the physical sensations linked to psychological distress. Therefore, this technique involves metaphorically removing what is choking the throat, causing pain in the stomach, or throwing off the burden in your shoulders. It aims to release trauma from the body, return it to the person or place where it was initially acquired, and to set a clear boundary.

Trauma and The Four Archetypes

Considering that most traumatic events occur in childhood, the little person experiencing the trauma might not have been able to escape the situation or assert themselves because it might have been impossible or too dangerous to do so. This means that they couldn't have set boundaries. As I've mentioned in Chapters 1 and 2, the Warrior energy is responsible for boundaries. This means that we should work on bringing the Warrior energy out of the Shadow through Shadow Work (Green, 2014). The Warrior will teach us where our boundaries should be and allow us to set them clearly, in cases where the circle of protection around us is either too big or too small.

Moreover, in traumatic situations, we often feel anger, grief, and fear. These emotions should be uncovered and released from the Shadow by working with our Lover energy. Another problem with childhood wounds is the lack of protection. We may have felt that no one was there to protect us or that the trauma wouldn't have happened if they hadn't abandoned us. To heal these, we need to work with our Sovereign energy and bring it out of the Shadow so as to build our self-esteem and self-love.

Finally, we may have internalized the perpetrator's voice and manifested it as our inner (merciless) judge. Therefore, we need to open a dialogue with our inner critic and transform it by working with our Magician energy that is in Shadow. This will give us a sense of peace, clarity, and strength.

Strategies to Release Emotional Pain

Here you'll find some simple yet effective strategies to release and cope with trauma.

1. Acknowledgment

It is common to minimize the traumatic event or deny it. Therefore, it is key to acknowledge that the event did happen and that it wasn't your fault. You can use the meditative techniques we talked about in Chapter 4 to observe the sensations in your body when you're feeling negative emotions caused by trauma. It is important to let yourself feel these emotions and acknowledge them in your safe space, where they can't harm you.

1. Self-Compassion

Not judging yourself is essential in this process since judgment can only cause guilt, shame, and more pain. Always treat yourself with utmost kindness, understanding, and respect. Keep in mind that there are no 'good' or 'bad' emotions; all of them help us understand ourselves and the world around us.

1. Acceptance

*A*ccepting your emotions doesn't mean that you're embracing your trauma or that what happened isn't bad. It just means that you accept that it has happened and that there is nothing, at this point, that you can do to change this fact. It also means that you will deal with it and stop suppressing it. Recognizing your emotions as valid, acceptable, and healthy is key to understanding why they're there and allowing you to move on.

1. Self-Expression

*L*earning how to express your emotions in a healthy way is essential. Meditation, journaling, dancing, yoga, etc., are a few constructive ways to express them. If you struggle with non-violent communication or interpersonal skills, there are many specialists and tools to help you gain awareness, be better informed and provide assistance to support you on your path.

1. Reclaiming Control

*C*hildhood trauma leaves us feeling helpless. This helplessness can carry on into adulthood, making us perpetual victims and causing us to keep making poor choices. Letting go of the old defenses you used as a child will help you reclaim control and heal.

Inner Child Healing

The Inner Child is the childlike aspect in our unconscious that takes over when we're faced with a challenge (Jacobson, 2017a). It is a subpersonality that has both positive and negative aspects while reflecting the child we once were. Moreover, it reflects some suppressed emotions that we were once taught are not acceptable if we want to be loved and accepted. It also reflects our unmet needs, innocence, creativity, and joy. Furthermore, it hides what we were taught by our environment about ourselves, like not being smart enough or only being good at certain things. Childhood trauma, especially, creates shame, which teaches us to hide our emotions in order to survive (Jacobson, 2017b). This is especially true in cases of childhood abuse, abandonment, and rejection. In particular, Inner Child Work can help with:

- Childhood abuse (mental, physical, or sexual)
- Anger issues
- Passive-aggressive behavior
- Low self-esteem
- Abandonment issues
- Emotional numbness
- Self-sabotage
- Self-criticism
- Difficulties with relationships
- Powerlessness
- Codependency

This concept is essential in Shadow Work because it helps you locate the roots of some of your adult problems, release repressed emotions, recognize unmet needs, resolve harmful patterns of thought and behavior, be more creative and playful, and raise your self-respect. Inner Child Work is about resolving the issues your inner child holds and uncovering their positive qualities (like joy, innocence, and confidence). It is about self-discovery: listening to, communicating with, and nurturing trauma. There are many forms Inner Child Work can take, such as:

- Visualizing and having a dialogue with your Inner Child.
- Journaling.
- Meditating to uncover and heal them.
- Learning to be your own parent.

There are many benefits to Inner Child Work, including being able to feel the things you were numb to before, setting personal boundaries, self-empowerment, developing your self-compassion and self-esteem, and gaining self-confidence.

How to Do Inner Child Work

The first thing you can do to begin Inner Child Work is to actually acknowledge your Inner Child's existence within you. You need to be open to exploring this relationship; doubting and resisting to explore the past will make it very hard for you to begin this process. Since the process is all about accepting and recognizing painful childhood experiences, bringing these into the light will help you understand their impact on your present and thus set a favorable foundation for your future.

Before we move on, please remember that most of these

steps are done with an open mind in a calm, meditative state, away from distractions.

So, as we said, number one: Visualize your inner child.

Secondly, you'll need to stop and listen carefully to your Inner Child so that you understand their feelings. These are, in truth, your own feelings at the point in time when you were wounded or affected by the traumatic event you are tackling. Your Inner Child's feelings will usually come up in situations that trigger strong emotions, discomfort, or unpleasant memories. These can include anger over unmet needs, abandonment, rejection, insecurity, vulnerability, guilt, shame, or anxiety. As such, you'll need to try and remember the events during your childhood from which these feelings originated and recall similar situations in your adulthood that trigger these responses. The goal of listening to the Inner Child's feelings is to identify them and stop repressing them.

The third thing you can do is open a conversation. My way of doing this is to visualize my current adult self reaching out and talking to myself as a child. This process is intense and personal, as you will usually need to tap into a specific memory of your child self-suffering or experiencing trauma. Some might prefer to write a letter to their Inner Child, others perhaps to draw pictures. In any case, this will allow you to open a dialogue and begin the healing process. This dialogue can include childhood memories explained from your present perspective as an adult. You can offer comfort and explain the reasons for situations that caused you pain as a child. You can also take note of how your Inner Child feels, how you can support them, and what they need from you at this point.

Once again, if you feel stuck, uncomfortable, or need to dig deeper, meditation is a great tool to use. It can help you answer the questions in the previous sentence and enable you to pay more attention to your emotions. This is key to noticing situations that trigger extreme reactions and dealing with unwanted emotions. Now, *this* is Shadow Work.

~

*Y*ou will find that another popular way of reaching out to your Inner Child is through journaling. This gives you the opportunity to sort through confusing experiences and recognize unhelpful patterns of thought or behavior that began in childhood.

Journaling

Journaling is a very powerful tool for Inner Child Work and Shadow Work. I have listed below a selection of prompts to help you begin with this process. (Stines, 2017)

Please note that the product of any prompt which requires you to write a letter to someone should remain for you only, as part of your healing journey; there is no need to actually give this person the letter.

*P*rompts for Inner Child Work

1. What areas of your life are causing you the most pain and concern? Describe how you feel about your early childhood.
2. Which emotional needs are you trying to fulfill for other people?

3. Which of your own needs are not being met right now?

4. Discuss the feelings you experience as a result of these unmet needs. After that, think back and write about the first time you remember feeling this unmet need and the emotions that came with it.

5. Write a list of individuals you are angry with and list your reasons. Think about whom you're most angry with and write them a deeply honest note or letter.

6. Now think about your unmet needs. Which of these do you believe you can't fulfill by yourself? What prevents you from doing so?

7. Write a list of the negative things you tell yourself. Then, flip the script; write another list that includes positive, self-accepting messages. This can be done little by little over time, for example by listing one new positive thought about yourself each day.

8. Write about your guilt and why you feel it. What triggers feelings of guilt and shame within you? Be as honest as can be. Then, reply to yourself in a kind, compassionate way, as if you were talking to a close friend.

9. Write the story of your childhood in the third person. Include its effects on your adult life. Then, read it aloud, imagining that this was written by a close friend or loved one. Reflect on how this new perspective helps you develop self-compassion and acceptance.

10. List the people you need to forgive and write a

letter to each of them explaining why you need to forgive them.

11. List the people you have wronged. Then, write a letter to each one of them asking for forgiveness.

12. List everyone you have unfinished emotional business with. Then write letters to them describing your feelings.

*P*rompts for Shadow Work

Here, you'll find some prompts for Shadow Work. You can note your answers in your journal and consider them at a later time.

- Which qualities bother me in others? Do I have those qualities and traits?

- What do I always complain about? Why?

- Which are my most toxic traits?

- What harmful behaviors do I wish I had more control over?

- Which need(s) do these behaviors satisfy?

- Which habits do I wish I could stop, and why?

- Write about the worst lie you've ever told.

- Write about the worst thing you've ever done.

- Write about whether you've apologized to someone you've hurt. Talk about why you did that or why not.

- Which aspect of my personality am I least proud of? Why?

- Which is my most painful memory?

- If I could travel back in time, what event(s) would I alter? Why?

- Write about traumas you've experienced as a teenager.

- Which of my friends am I envious of? Why?

- Write about a time when you might have stepped over someone else to get ahead. Talk about how this made you feel.

- Who or what irritates me and why?

- What am I most selfish about?

- Am I ever intentionally rude? Why?

- How do I act when I'm angry? How does that make me feel about myself?

- Am I a good or a bad person?

- Which negative emotions do I wish I could experience less often?

- What are my inner demons? How do they affect my life?

- If I had an addiction, what would I be addicted to and why?

- Write about the last time you fought with a family member. What was the fight about and what triggered it?

- Do you think you're better than others? Why or why not?

- What is my unfulfilled desire in life?

- List two negative traits of yours that you'd like to work on. What would change if you worked on them?

- Do I have a favorite parent? Why or why not?

- What am I most afraid of and why?

- What are my phobias? How did they start?

- How do I feel about sex? How does it affect me emotionally?

- Have I ever been sexually/emotionally/physically aggressive with someone?

- What does being lazy mean for me? Is it okay to be lazy? Why or why not?

- Have I ever deeply hated anyone? Do I still hate them? Why?

- What is the most embarrassing thing that's ever happened to me?

- What do I secretly judge in others? Why?

- What do I try to get from others?

- If I could swap lives with someone else, who would that be and why?

- Who's the biggest negative influence in my life? Why?

- Write about one of your greatest regrets.

- Who am I holding grudges against? Why?

- Am I able to forgive myself for my mistakes? Why or why not?

*P*rompts for Both Inner Child Work and Shadow Work

(Tropeaka, 2019)

- How I am spending my days now will be how I spend my days from here on out. How does that make me feel?

- Describe how an ideal day would start.

- What are the positives of being triggered unexpectedly? How can I use triggers to my advantage?

- What am I most proud of in my life right now?

- What are the recurring problems in my life? What would happen if I viewed them as opportunities?

- Are what I want and what I need the same?

- Write about a time when a rejection pointed you to the right direction, that is when you gained an opportunity or positive result from being rejected.

- What am I most excited about in my future? What am I looking forward to?

- When I feel stressed, what am I resisting?

- Given that I can't change anyone, how can I lead by example?

- When I feel depressed, what is the purpose I've lost?

- Do I listen to my heart or do I use my mind to analyze situations? Why?

- In which circumstances do I feel the happiest?

- What do I want recognition for?

- What do I wish others understood about me?

- What does freedom mean to me? What does it look and feel like?

- In which situations do I feel most valued and loved?

- What am I most afraid of, in regard to my future?

- Who is my true self? Who am I outside of social constructs?

- Have my values changed over the past few years? If so, how? Why?

Other Techniques for Inner Dialogue

Automatic Writing

Automatic writing means writing from the unconscious. It requires you not to form conscious thoughts when writing so that what spills out is non-judgmental and non-critical. The point is to keep writing, even if your sentences are unfinished, ungrammatical, and don't align in a cohesive way. In Shadow Work, automatic writing is a valuable tool that helps you express your thoughts and emotions as you're experiencing them (Camp, 2017). This stream-of-consciousness writing shows you your unfiltered Self while also demonstrating your thought process, as it happens. To do this, you can sit with a pen and paper and recall a past situation associated with what you want to work on. For example, if you want to work on your feelings of shame, try to remember a shameful situation from your past. Visualize it and try to recall the memory and all the senses associated with it. Then, while still visualizing, start writing as fast as possible without looking at what you're writing or stopping.

You can take this a step further and reply to a question with 10 answers. For instance, if you're working on your social anxiety, give 10 responses to the question "Why am I afraid of social situations?". You can rephrase this question according to the emotion, thought, or behavior on which you're working.

Active Imagination

Active Imagination aims at having a conversation with the unconscious part of yourself (Johnson, 1992). It is like a dream, but you're fully awake and in control of the fantasy, in contrast to dreaming. It involves allowing images to rise from the unconscious so that they come into your imagination as they would appear in your dreams. Then, you can talk and interact with these images as they reveal things that you never consciously knew or thought. This means that they might divulge beliefs or opinions that look nothing like yours. These images are symbols that represent parts of yourself that are buried deep, which means that they symbolize the contents of your unconscious.

In fact, Jung considered Active Imagination more important than dreams because he found them to be a more effective path to the unconscious. That is because in dreams, the conscious mind cannot participate, whereas in Active Imagination, the conscious mind can participate in the events. It is also a form of meditation.

Active Imagination is also different from passive imagination, in that passive fantasy is daydreaming without consciously participating. An example of Active Imagination is something we all do: self-talk. If we're feeling worried, we might confront our worry in our imagination, engage in a dialogue with it, and discover our internal conflict. By resolving conflict, we piece together the parts of ourselves that were fragmented. So, this way, our ego and parts of the unconscious can communicate, which brings about peace and a sense of wholeness.

It is important to note that dreaming decreases dramatically when you engage in Active Imagination because you learn to assimilate the contents of the unconscious before they have a chance to come up in dreams. Sometimes, when you're doing Active Imagination, your dreams might also become more focused and less repetitive.

Before starting with Active Imagination, you need to

decide how you'll record it. You should keep notes about your inner dialogues because it helps you stay focused on what you're doing rather than wandering off into daydreaming. You can use a notebook to write by hand and abbreviate to indicate who is talking. For example, you can use an 'E' for 'ego' and a 'W' for 'woman' if you're talking with a woman. You could also use your computer if it suits you better. If you choose to use your computer, you can write lowercase letters to record what you're saying and uppercase letters to record what the other person is saying. Keep in mind that you don't need to stop and make corrections (as in Automatic Writing) in spelling, punctuation, grammar, or syntax. If you feel a strong need to make them, you can proofread and edit it afterward so that you don't shift your focus.

If you don't feel comfortable writing, you can use other forms of expression like painting, dancing, acting out the dialogue, sculpting, music, etc. The important thing is that you record your inner dialogues somehow and that you are the only person reading them. It is also essential to find a quiet space for Active Imagination sessions. This should be a space where you're alone and where you can express yourself freely.

So, after you've decided the medium with which you'll record your sessions and found a place to do that, it is time to begin. There are four steps to the Active Imagination process. These are not exactly the same for everyone, but most people successfully go through these during Active Imagination sessions.

The first step is the Invitation. This means that you invite the 'beings' in your unconscious mind to make contact with you. It is better if you do this during meditation so that you can take your mind off the external world and focus on your imagination. You can go to a place (either real or imaginative) and try to describe it vividly so that you immerse yourself in it and see who you'll encounter. It's important to note that the invitation is challenging for some people at first. If this happens to you, be patient and don't give up trying. It will come to you eventually. Remember that when someone comes to you during these sessions, they won't necessarily say or do what you expect. They might catch you completely off guard and surprise you.

If you are comfortable in meditation, you can follow this process by waiting on alert. This means that you clear your mind of all thoughts, go to the quiet location we talked about before, and simply wait to see who will show up. This, however, requires more concentration and patience. When a figure appears within your mind, you mustn't reject it or judge it. Just see what it has to say. Once you see the figure, you can ask them who they are, what they want, etc. If this doesn't work, you can use your fantasies. This means that you turn passive fantasy into Active Imagination by reliving parts of your day and choosing an image, person, or situation to focus on. Then you use this place to start the process by participating in the fantasy and consciously conversing with the characters.

Another thing you can do is visit symbolic places. This means that you settle into your imagination and wait to see if you meet anyone. Furthermore, you can use personifications, meaning that you choose an image to represent your feelings. You can go into your imagination and ask for the feeling to reveal itself. You are basically free to roam as you please – it is, after all, your own mind.

Finally, engaging in a dialogue with dream figures is

another idea to get you started. This is a technique that views Active Imagination as extended dreams, meaning that you are 'continuing' the dream in your imagination, resolving issues within. You can also dialogue with figures you've seen in dreams.

I view this process as a half-hypnosis; by tapping into the unconscious, we remain present yet detached enough to perceive things we otherwise would not.

The second step is the Dialogue. After the images have risen, you can begin communicating with them. The point here is to vent what comes to mind. Even if the figure doesn't speak to you, you can start the conversation by asking who they are, what they want, what they would like to talk about, or what they would like to do. This process focuses on listening to the figures instead of arguing with them, so questions help a lot with that. If, after you've tried to initiate a conversation, the figure doesn't really respond, you can express your feelings about them. If they remind you of another person or situation, or even in the event that you find yourself feeling afraid of them, you can let them know.

Do not forget to record everything. Try to stick with one figure at a time until the conflict is resolved. Then, you can move on to others during a different session. It is essential to be in touch with your feelings in this process. When feelings arise (and I can assure you they will), let them surface as they are. Address them as you would a real person in an actual conversation without exerting control. Being detached will lead to passive imagination, unlocking parts of your Shadow.

Moreover, learning to listen is necessary for having a dialogue. Listening means that we let go of resistance. No arguing with figures that seem hostile or that you don't like! Accepting what is remains essential to unlocking suppressed issues and stopping the never-ending cycle of ego conflict. Conflicts aren't resolved with hostility. Instead, we need to accept that these are part of ourselves, and we need to get to know them. This is especially true for Shadow figures that we have deemed 'bad' for years.

Active Imagination for Shadow Work requires us to listen even to the 'bad' figures. Eventually, you will be able to learn to reply and contribute to these dialogues openly. It will be most beneficial for you to share your own information, viewpoint, and values. This way, both the ego and the unconscious treat each other as equals. Remember to avoid manipulating the figures. This can happen instinctively, as some of this work will be painful, and your psyche will try to protect you, as it always has. Avoid planning what they'll say or attempt to dominate them – this would be extremely counterproductive.

The third step is about Values. The creatures in your Active Imagination represent the force of the universe, and thus, you are responsible for the Active Imagination's moral, ethical, and practical elements. This means that the burden of taking an ethical stance so that there is balance in conflicts falls on you. For example, if one of your inner figures tells you to do something that is against your values, you don't have to do it. In addition, refuse to allow one archetype to take over at the expense of others, and always make sure to preserve your human values.

The final step is about Rituals. Rituals help you bring the experience of Active Imagination into your daily life. They can be either a physical act (like straightening out a relationship) or a symbolic act (such as burying an object related to an obsession): your journey, your pick.

· · ·

Internal Family Systems

Internal Family Systems (IFS) aims to locate the different parts of you that are causing difficulties in your life or holding you back in order to heal and unify them (Early, 2009). IFS views these different parts as divisions in the psyche or subpersonalities that have their own emotions and motivations. In this view, the Inner Child is one of our parts. Moreover, these parts frequently shift, meaning that one part may take over for a while before another comes in. This usually presents as slight changes in mood. They get activated at certain times, in certain circumstances. For example, when mingling with a large group of people, you may suddenly feel shy or uncomfortable and want to leave.

The presence of a subpersonality is indicated by changes in reactions, thought sequences, behavior patterns, and body sensations. IFS is consistent with the Jungian view of the Self as the center of our being. It supports the idea that hurt, trauma, and shame force us to unconsciously create inner characters that take over to protect our psyche.

IFS aims to facilitate access to the Self, like the Jungian notion of Individuation, through healing and connecting the different parts. Furthermore, the different parts hold qualities that have been lost due to childhood trauma. It also aims at teaching the parts to cooperate with one another.

At the center of this theory is the idea that all of our subpersonalities have positive intentions towards us, ranging from protection to making us feel good or avoid pain. Nevertheless, some parts seem stuck in negative patterns, which can be destructive (like addictions). Although they may sometimes take extreme stances or unwise decisions, they are doing what they think is best for you. They might be doing this because their perception of certain situations is distorted, such as exaggerated danger. Some of them are stuck in the defense mechanisms they once used to protect you as a child, which now seems immature or ineffective.

Here are some of the different roles subpersonalities can take.

*P*rotectors

These seek to protect us from feeling pain. They try to keep us in our comfort zone so that we don't experience pain, fear, or shame. They do this either by repressing our discomfort so that we don't feel it or by arranging our lives in a way that we won't feel pain. Protectors are the most accessible and the first we encounter when exploring the different parts of ourselves. They are influenced by the events or relationships of our childhoods that involve abandonment, betrayal, judgment, or abuse. Hence, they will do everything to avoid situations that are similar to those we experienced as children.

Protectors can be viewed as the defenses we use to cope with pain, such as addictions, overeating, or excessive self-criticism (to avoid judgment from others). On a more positive side, Protectors can help us build confidence and self-esteem, particularly when it comes to gaining popularity or success.

So, to get to know your protectors, you can think of two of them and answer the following questions for each one:

1. How do they help me manage my life?
2. How do they help me interact with the world?
3. How do they relate to others?

4. How do they protect me from pain?
5. What is their positive intent?
6. What are they trying to protect me from?

*E*xiles

Exiles are parts of ourselves that are in pain from our childhoods. In fact, they're in so much pain that the protectors try to shield us from them. Moreover, Exiles are stuck at a specific age such as two, five, or seven years old, whichever time during childhood when something traumatic happened that we couldn't process because we lacked the resources. Exiles aren't always stuck in just one specific moment; some might be stuck in a situation that lasted many years (such as an ongoing toxic relationship with a parent). They often adopt the beliefs of our families and can be affected by incidents that were beyond the family's control, like a war or illness. Exiles can exhibit a wide variety of painful emotions such as fear of abandonment, criticism, and being shamed while also holding beliefs about us or the world (like being unlovable). Consequently, they are pushed away by the protector due to all this pain they're holding. To learn more about your exiles, answer the following questions for each Exile:

1. Which emotions does my Exile feel?
2. What pain do they carry?
3. What are they afraid of?
4. What are their negative beliefs?
5. Where are they stuck (situation or relationship from childhood)?

6. What situations trigger them?
7. What protectors come up when this happens?

The Self

As Jung's theory suggests, the Self is our core and embodies who we truly are. The true center of our being is grounded, centered, non-reactive, and calm. It doesn't get triggered by external factors, even in challenging circumstances. Although all of us have glimpsed our true Self, our more extreme subpersonalities tend to repress it because of their prevalence. As a matter of fact, they are so prevalent that we end up identifying with them, inadvertently even becoming them, while losing touch with the Self.

In IFS, the Self is the agent of psychological healing because it seeks to connect with the other parts and heal them. The Self has four main qualities:

1. Connectedness. It feels close to other people and harmoniously relates to them. Moreover, it seeks connection with our other parts.
2. Curiosity. The Self is curious about other people and other parts without seeking to judge them. It wants to understand them and find out why they act in a certain way, their positive intent, and what they're trying to protect us from.
3. Compassion. It naturally feels compassion towards other people and other subpersonalities. Furthermore, it wants to support and understand them. It cares about the pain of the exiles and feels compassion for protectors.

4. Calmness. The Self is calm and centered, which supports you when witnessing and healing parts.

The Process

To begin the process, you need to choose a protector to work on. You should start with a protector because you don't want to rush to the exiles since protectors want to protect them. Gaining the protector's trust is important in getting to know the exiles. If the protectors are healed, they will be less defensive and allow their positive qualities to emerge. Furthermore, they can be accessed more easily because they are part of the conscious mind.

The first thing to do is think about a situation that upsets you, for example, feeling shy and wanting to withdraw when you're in large groups of people. Then, you will observe the feelings that this situation causes you (like anger or sadness) and your attitudes associated with it (such as being judgmental or doubtful). Another important factor to consider is bodily sensations, such as stomach aches or dizziness.

Moreover, observing your thoughts about yourself or others is essential. Thoughts can become thought patterns, which should also be considered through this process. For instance, the thought "My boss is intrusive" can become the thought pattern of obsessing over a difficult conversation with her. Noticing your behavior (such as withdrawing) or ongoing behavior patterns linked to this thought is also useful. Lastly, desires should also be taken into account. All these indicate the presence of a part. A few simple steps to getting to know a part include choosing one part and writing down:

1. The name of the part.
2. When it is activated (describe the situation).
3. What it feels like (emotions).
4. What it looks like.
5. How it feels in your body (physical sensations).
6. What it says.
7. How it behaves.
8. What it wants.

So, the first part of this process requires you to get to know the protector. To do that, choose a quiet place and enter into a meditative state, as we've talked about in Chapter 4.

Then, you'll want to conjure up the emotions, images, body sensations, and internal voice associated with the protector. It's okay if you can't feel all these at once. Try to focus, instead, on what you *can* feel. If the part you're trying to access is activated, your job will be easier. If the part isn't activated, you can try to recall a moment when it was at the forefront and try to remember the feelings, body sensations, images, and inner voice of this part. Write down what you're experiencing using the above list.

To recap, you must pick a situation that causes negative thoughts, reactions, and feelings and try to tap into them. Then, it will be essential that you try to bring in the Self – your Self - in order to remain a detached observer and refrain from criticizing those parts. This means that you will have to remain centered and grounded. As you now know, meditation will be of great help with this.

The next step is to check for blending. In other words, you'll need to feel, observe, and determine how much you relate to the part right now. To do that, you will need to consider the following questions:

1. How much of their emotions are you feeling? If you're not feeling their emotions very strongly, then you can proceed to a constructive dialogue with them.

2. How much of their perspective do you buy into? Or, which of their beliefs do you tend to adopt? A part might be telling you something that isn't true (that your spouse doesn't love you, for example). It is necessary to assess to what extent you really agree with this perspective.

3. How much distance do you have from this part? Can you witness their emotions and beliefs? If you have some distance from the part, then this indicates that the Self is in the forefront, which is the best place to start.

4. What are your feelings towards this part? Do you like it or hate it? This question helps you determine if you're blended with it. This means that if you give a clear answer to this question, then you are not really blended with the part.

If you establish that you are blended with the part, you can now choose to work with it.

The third step is to check if you're actually in the Self. After checking whether you're separate enough, it is time to ask yourself what your feelings are towards this part. You mustn't label the part as either good, bad, harmful, or helpful. Instead, you need to consider what your attitude is towards this part here and now. For example, if you're feeling pity towards a sad part, you need to sit with this pity. Then, you should approach this attitude with curiosity. Why are you feeling pity? Why is the part sad? Curiosity, openness, compassion, and acceptance are attitudes you'll be holding if you're connected with the Self, and this will be your cue to move on to the next step.

If you're feeling negative emotions towards this part, such as anger, judgment, or fear, this means that you're blended with another part, and you will need to unblend. Usually, this part concerned with meeting the target part is a protector. It is then a good idea to work with the concerned part first. To do so, you can access it and ask what its concerns are. Try to understand what is happening within, be present, and show empathy. Explain why you need this part to step aside. Reassure them that you'll handle the situation carefully, and tell them that they'll only need to step back for this session.

The fourth step is to discover the protector's role. You'll want to get to know their emotions, concerns, beliefs, and role in your life. It is very helpful if you ask questions to the protector. You can lead with the following:

1. What do you feel?
2. What are your concerns?
3. What's your role, and how do you perform it?
4. What do you want to accomplish with this role?
5. What are you afraid of happening if you didn't do this?
6. What makes you so angry?
7. How do you relate to others?
8. How do you interact with the other parts?
9. How do you feel about [emotion]?
10. How do you feel about [situation] (like approaching others)?
11. What do you want?

12. What emotions would come up if you didn't play this role?
13. How long have you been the protector?
14. What do you want from me?

At this point, try to notice their body sensations, emotions, and image (how they look physically). As absurd as this can seem, it will help go deeper into this healing process.

Additionally, you might know something about them without them telling you. For example, you might know directly that this part is distrustful, without you feeling the distrust or them telling you.

Then, you might want to name the part. The name can be anything, like one that describes it (Controlling Part), a real name (like Paul), or from a character (Buddha). It is better if your part chooses their own name rather than you naming them. Furthermore, you can find out whether the protector offers external or internal protection, that is, whether they are protecting the vulnerable exiles from being harmed by others (external) or trying to protect you from feeling the exiles' emotions (internal).

Lastly, when you're ending a session, make sure to thank the part for making themselves known to you and let them know that you'll finish your work with them in another session (if your work is unfinished). Build a trusting relationship with them and show them appreciation for their positive intent in order to fulfill the final step of building a trusting relationship. Tell them that you understand and appreciate them.

~

*W*e will now move on to the parts that are related to the Shadow. These parts, concealed within the Shadow, are hidden from awareness. Therefore, you can start working with them once you've gained the protectors' trust. Then, ask permission from them to work with the parts they're protecting. If you don't have permission to work with the exile, then the protector will interrupt the work. Before you start working with an exile, you need to get an idea of who they are. To do this, you can think about the protector's answer to the question, "What are you afraid will happen if you didn't do this?". Their answer will point to an exile they're protecting. For instance, if they say that they think you'll be scared, then your exile is feeling this emotion.

Then, ask the protector for permission. The first step is to access the exile. To do this, contact them the same way you contacted the protector. The second step is to unblend from them. Exiles sometimes tend to flood you with pain (blending) so that they are heard. You need to stay in the Self and relate to the exile; not become it. Ask the exile not to flood you with their emotions and explain you can only help them if you remain in the Self. In other words, ask them to show you their feelings and keep them separate from you, rather than make you feel them.

The third step is to unblend from affected parts. To do this, kindly ask the part to step aside and explain that you're only trying to help the exile. If you observe that the protector is concerned because the exile has previously caused problems, explain that you won't let the exile take over and that you want to heal the exile. If the protector is judgmental towards the exile because they think they are too weak, explain to the protector that being vulnerable is not the exile's fault. They most likely only feel like this because of what happened to them during childhood.

Move gently through this process, and remember to stay connected to your breath.

The fourth step is to learn more about the exile. Ask the exile what makes them feel so sad and keep asking them questions to get to know them, just like you did with the protector.

The final step is to build a trusting relationship with them, which is achieved through showing compassion to them.

Now that you have gotten to know the exiles and protectors, you need to access their childhood origins. In other words, you must find out when they were formed and in response to what. If you recall, while you were getting to know the exile, you asked them which situations in the present trigger them. Well, once you've built a trusting relationship, you can ask them what caused them to form. A few ideas on how to do this are:

1. Ask them to show you a memory or image of what happened to make you feel these emotions during childhood.
2. Ask them to show when they first took this role.
3. Ask them to show you how they learned to believe this.

Avoid looking for specific, complete memories. Keep in mind that you might only get fragments, images, or body sensations. Moreover, they might not want to show you the memory in order to protect you. If this happens, reassure them that you are an adult now and can handle more. When the exile shows you the memory, be compassionate and understanding; show them that you'll be there with them and that you understand their pain.

It is important to mention here that the inner child is an exile. In order for the exile to heal, you need to reparent them. This means you need to enter the traumatic memory alongside the exile/inner child. Remember that you need to be in or connected to the Self in order to do this successfully. In this situation, be with the exile as a loving parent would accompany their child through a difficult time. Show them that you care and support them through thick and thin.

Generally, reparenting is a technique that has to do with taking the role of a concerned and trustworthy parent (Jacobson, 2018a). It is based on the idea of the Inner Child's needs not being met during childhood. Reparenting offers you the opportunity to be vulnerable, learn about your hidden needs and how to meet them, and learn to trust. More than anything, it sets a foundation for healing through developing an unconditional love towards yourself.

Reparenting is particularly helpful for psychological issues arising from unmet needs and childhood trauma. These includes:

- Trust issues
- Child abuse
- Relationship problems
- Low self-esteem
- Anger management issues

Moreover, you can benefit from reparenting if your parent

was aloof, extremely stressed, controlling, disciplined you harshly, or had a mental illness. This technique will help you better understand yourself and others, as well as gain some perspective and empathy towards your parents. Children who are raised in these conditions often develop coping strategies that are unhelpful in adulthood. Therefore, this work focuses on acceptance, letting go, and forgiveness – towards ourselves and others. In short, reparenting will allow you to start healing deeply rooted wounds from your childhood.

Everyone has wounds to heal linked to their upbringing. These are diverse and vary in the type of impact they have in later years. A common wound is linked to feeling unloved. When their Inner Child feels unloved, they seek to cling to relationships with people who have their own problems and, more importantly, cannot contain their toxicity. They end up depending on these unhealed (at times harmful) individuals, gaining self-worth only by pleasing them. In some cases, we become so afraid of being dependent on anyone that we don't trust others or avoid committing to a relationship.

People whose Inner Child feels unloved need to consider what sort of relationships and friendships they're engaged in, as well as what their core beliefs are about love. Do you feel like you are sabotaging or blocking love? Do you believe love doesn't exist? In what ways are you trying to obtain love? Are you manipulating, clinging, or begging for love? If these statements and questions describe you, then your Inner Child might require healing in the area of self-love.

The second thing we might lack is structure. This can manifest as being completely unorganized, missing appointments, and being messy despite our best efforts. If this sounds like you, try to keep note of what you do during the day. This can be as precise as writing down what you do during each hour. This short-term activity will help you observe your patterns.

The third wound has to do with limits, which is related to not being able to set healthy boundaries or not having the ability to say no. As a result, you might constantly feel exhausted from trying to please others or live up to others' expectations.

Another common wound is linked to identity. This means you have no idea who you really are because you're always trying to be who others want you to be.

Next, a lack of guidance will manifest as being indecisive, not knowing what you want, doing what other people tell you, and feeling angry or regretful after. You might not be able to recognize your own needs or desires.

The final aspect of inner-child wounds revolves around self-acceptance. This means that you're very self-critical and stuck in negative thought patterns.

As you might have observed, most of these wounds are interconnected on some level. They are complex and diverse, just as each individual's upbringing and life path is. As such, a holistic approach to healing, with Shadow Work at the center, is the best way to begin this journey.

Now that you've learned how to accept and release trauma, including Inner Child healing, journaling, Automatic Writing, Active Imagination, and Internal Family Systems, it is time to move on to the next chapter, which will provide you with more practical tools for Shadow Work.

7

EMBRACING WHOLENESS

 Shadow work is the path of the heart warrior.

— CARL G. JUNG

*O*nce you begin going through the motions of Shadow Work, you'll feel different. A new, self-directed life will reveal itself to you. The new you will have learned self-compassion and self-acceptance and will be able to move forward with self-actualization. Nevertheless, you must continue working on your self-acceptance, even after Shadow Work. In fact, I'm not entirely convinced there ever is an actual "after Shadow Work." Perhaps this is simply growth, a slow, beautiful, ever-changing process by which we tenderly mend our soul and live true to ourselves.

Always remember to challenge the 'good' part of your-self. Many of us have learned to see ourselves as good and highlight our positive qualities. Unfortunately, this conditioning has created a split in our psyche, making us disown other parts of ourselves that don't fit this narrative. Often buried within the Shadow, these disowned parts influence our behavior and challenge our "good" parts.

To get to know your disowned parts, you can make a list of all your positive qualities. After that, try to identify within yourself their opposites. For example, if you believe that you are a hard-working person, try to identify areas of laziness that you might have repressed, thus ending up in the Shadow. As you know by now, to grow and heal, you will need to accept this part and recognize that it's there for a reason. Maybe avoiding being lazy at all costs leaves you emotionally and physically exhausted. Because you believe you're not lazy, you might think that to rest implies being lazy and, therefore, avoid resting. This is non-acceptance of Self is what we are trying to heal. Self-love begins with accepting ourselves fully, exactly as we are. Accepting and embracing our flaws can lead to a clearer perspective, better-defined goals, and more significant accomplishments in all spheres of life.

On the other hand, you most likely have genuine positive qualities in your Shadow, like being creative. Perhaps, at some point in your life, you were forced to repress this creativity for one reason or another. This is what we call the "Golden Shadow," or the 'Gold.' Projection has its place in this too. Usually, we tend to admire others who possess the gold we're repressing. We've talked about projection in Chapter 5, but only as it relates to the things that bother us in others (therefore within ourselves). Now that we've navigated the workings of the Shadow let's have a look at the traits that we actually admire in others. What qualities or attributes do you particularly value in others? Which of these do you yearn for or make you feel slightly envious? For a moment, consider whether you might be repressing some traits that you admire in others. Positive traits that, for some reason, you have not allowed yourself to feel, disclose, or experience. Maybe you secretly wish you could be more like your sibling, a creative free-thinker, or wonder why you are incapable of being like that, of embracing such detachment from judgment.

Shadow Work can help mend the Golden Shadow and lead you to uncover your true potential. When you catch yourself wishing to be more like someone you admire, ask yourself when the last time was that you exhibited this quality. What happened then? Were you put down? Were you rejected? How did you end up believing that this trait is not already a part of you?

By uncovering the reasons and thought patterns that led you to believe that you are not the thing you value, you can set in motion the destruction of old habits. You can start to alter those inhibiting thought patterns and begin to experience being that which you admire and genuinely want to be. Rediscover these qualities within you, the ones you've repressed, and greet them with love.

Below you'll find an exercise to help you with both types of qualities that reside in Shadow:

1. Choose a person you have difficulty with or feel obsessed with/attracted to.
2. Imagine this person and write down their qualities, those that upset you or those you admire. Use the third person pronoun.
3. Talk to them. Have a dialogue with this person in

your imagination and use the second person pronoun. Tell them what bothers you or what you love about them. If you don't like this person, ask them about:

- Why they are doing this.
- What they want from you.
- What they're trying to show you.
- What they want to teach you.

4. If you admire this person, ask them about:

- Why they are so good, kind, generous, etc.
- What they want to achieve by being good, kind, generous.
- What they're trying to show you.
- What they want to teach you.

Imagine their response, speak it out loud, and write it down in your journal. Become this person. Try to embody the traits summoned in step 2, using the first person pronoun, such as "I am angry" or "I am kind."

Notice these qualities in yourself. Allow yourself to experience these traits and re-own them.

During this process, it is essential to be completely honest with yourself and be able to sit in discomfort, as both of these are required in this process. Keep in mind that your Shadow is a web of your past; it is not who you are, nor the whole of your potential self. It is a part of you that is hidden, one you can uncover in order to be whole. Keep in mind that it doesn't define your identity. For example, if you have repressed revengefulness, this doesn't mean that all you are is revengeful. It is just a part of you, one small piece of the puzzle. Remember that the end goal is to integrate the part of yourself you've hidden in order to embrace self-love and live more authentically. After all, self-acceptance means that you accept all of yourself.

≈

*N*ow, let's indulge in more healing journaling. Over the following few pages, you'll find a few prompts writing exercises to help you move forward on your journey.

Gratitude Writing

As you might know, I am an immense advocate for nurturing a practice of gratitude. This way of thinking and being is life-changing, potentially altering your physical and mental health, as well as allowing you to manifest abundance in all shapes and forms.

Gratitude writing is a practice that involves recognizing the things you are grateful for in the past, present, and future. You might choose to look back on a memory from a holiday you particularly enjoyed or a special moment shared with loved ones. You can take a moment to breathe and ground yourself. Find gratitude in being healthy and at peace right here and now. You can also choose to be grateful for a mistake that led you to more clarity and direction in your life. The options are endless, and the healing power of this practice is immense. Doing this for a few minutes each day will also help you accept things as they are, reduce pessimism, and enable you to develop a more optimistic mindset.

Future Self Writing

This type of journaling will help you change deep-rooted behaviors and set intentions for your future self by creating conscious awareness of your behavior patterns. It is a practice that can also assist with your Inner Child work.

Future Self Writing will take about 15 minutes daily, a moment that can easily be incorporated into your self-care routine. The notion of Future Self is quite self-explanatory: it is about how you see yourself in the future.

Now, the first step to this practice is about self-awareness and focusing on behavioral patterns you want to change. In your journal, reflect on and answer one question or statement each day:

1. What behavior do I want to change?
2. How would I be different if I didn't have this behavior?
3. How will I practice the new behaviors?

For example, if your answer to the first question is that you want to stop being defensive, then the answer to the second question would be that you would be able to consider different perspectives or connect more easily with others. Then, in the third question, you would say that you want to start observing your feelings and thoughts when they arise instead of reacting to them impulsively.

After answering the questions, start implementing these changes in your daily life. Allow some time before proceeding to the next behavior. As for the second step, write about the following:

1. Today I will focus on the pattern of:
2. In the future, I will experience more:
3. How do I feel about who I am becoming?

8

EMERGENCE

 Only in darkness can you see the stars.

— MARTIN LUTHER KING JR.

*S*hadow Work is an incredibly challenging yet equally rewarding life-long journey. It is inner work at its finest, a tumultuous path of self-discovery that ultimately leads to *you*.

Now that you have taken the leap - whether concretely or contemplatively – and have begun to ponder and explore the vastness within, you can begin to heal your wounds and live your truest, most fulfilling life, grounded on a solid foundation of Self.

You are now in the process of personal transformation, moving from childhood to adulthood. You were taught a set of beliefs and rules that you are now transcending and breaking free from in order to discover your true self. The first stage was the departure when you left the safety of the conscious to enter the unconscious. You bravely left behind what is known and safe to you: your comfort zone. Then, you moved on to the second stage of initiation, only to uncover some of your inner demons and be tested. Perhaps you faced them and discovered a newfound sense of peace; perhaps you will try again tomorrow.

Along the way, you might come across allies, enemies, or mentors. You must find the strength to let go of safety and find your way to the third stage of return, meaning that you will have internally transformed through experience. This is your return home. You have embraced the unknown, and you should be grateful to yourself for summoning such strength and willpower.

Always remember that perceived problems are opportunities for growth. They give you the chance to overcome setbacks, limitations, and condition behavior. Challenges create internal tension. These conflicts cause a disharmony so tumultuous for the psyche that it forces us into action and, ultimately, resolution. So, accept the call and embark on the journey. Find the answers within you. It is important to do this work at your own pace and not force specific outcomes. Pressure will lead to ignoring important cues and making your Shadow denser. The steps presented here take different amounts of time for each one of us to navigate, and your own rhythm must be observed and respected.

Navigating this work, you'll be rewarded with less fatigue and lethargy. These grow in us due to the heavy burdens of our unprocessed emotions and traumas that we carry. These burdens can even cause physical pain and disease. Inner strength as a result of Shadow Work also gives you a greater sense of balance, a sense of being centered. Integration of our suppressed parts, emotions, and traits is a truly rewarding process.

Embrace each cycle of growth and each step towards self-discovery. Don't forget that Shadow Work is a personal process. The boon or reward is there and will come in time. You'll slowly begin to notice your relationships improving by being more grounded, human, and whole. Accepting your darker parts means accepting the darker parts in others, too. Once you begin naturally feeling more compassionate, kind, and loving towards others, you can be sure of one thing: these elements are already deep-rooted within you. Remember: what we feel and project onto others is a reflection of our inner landscape. Accepting things as they are, feeling more energized, being less triggered...these are all a reflection of our healing and inner peace.

 our true self is right here, continually looking for opportunities to emerge. Keep facing your darkness; freedom awaits on the other side.

POSTSCRIPT

We'd love to hear your thoughts…
Please leave a review!

As an independent author with a small marketing budget, **reviews** are my livelihood on this platform. If you enjoyed this book, I would truly appreciate if you left your honest feedback. You can do this by clicking the link to *Embracing Your Darkness* at amazon.com.

Additionally, you can jump in and join our well-being community via https://www.facebook.com/groups/theemeraldsociety, or contact me directly at ydgardens@emeraldsocpublishing.com.

I personally read every single review and it warms my heart to hear from my readers.

With Kindness,

Yas

SOME RESOURCES

Here you'll find some books that I've found very helpful on my own Shadow Work journey:

Tolle, E. (2004). *The Power of Now: A guide to spiritual enlightenment*. New World Library.

Singer, M. A. (2007). *The Untethered Soul: The journey beyond yourself.* New Harbinger Publishing.

Brown, B. (2010). *The Gifts of Imperfection: Let go of who you think you're supposed to be and embrace who you are*. Hazelden Publishing.

Bly, R. (1988). *A Little Book on The Human Shadow.* HarperOne.

Byron, K. (2017). *A Mind at Home with Itself: How asking four questions can free your mind, open your heart, and turn your world around*. HarperOne.

REFERENCES

Barry, C., & Blandford, M. A. (n.d.). *Shadow Work Basics* [Audio File]. Shadow Work. Retrieved December 5, 2021, from https://shadowwork.com/

Blundell, A. (2019, November 12). *More Self-Critical Than You Realise? 11 Signs to Spot.* Harley Therapy Blog. https://www.harleytherapy.co.uk/counselling/self-critical-signs.htm

Byron, K. (n.d.). *Do The Work.* The Work of Byron Katie. Retrieved December 7, 2021, from https://thework.com/instruction-the-work-byron-katie/

Camp, S. (2017, December 12). *The Definitive Guide to Shadow Work Using Jungian Psychology.* Unstoppable Rise. https://www.unstoppablerise.com/shadow-work-on-shadow-self/

Centre of Excellence. (2019, September 16). *What is Shadow Work?* Centre of Excellence. https://www.centreofexcellence.com/what-is-shadow-work/

Cherry, K. (2020). *The 4 Major Jungian Archetypes.*

Verywell Mind. https://www.verywellmind.com/what-are-jungs-4-major-archetypes-2795439

Chopra Addiction and Wellness Center. (2019, October 21). *5 Strategies to Release and Overcome Emotional Pain.* Chopra Treatment Center for Alcohol & Drug Addiction Rehab in BC. http://www.chopratreatmentcenter.com/blog/2019/10/21/5-strategies-release-overcome-emotional-pain/

Chopra, D., Ford, D., & Williamson, M. (2011). *The Shadow Effect: Illuminating the hidden power of your true self.* HarperOne.

Davy, J. (n.d.). *What Happens After the Trauma?* Leader Letter. Retrieved December 10, 2021, from http://www.wright.edu/~scott.williams/LeaderLetter/trauma.htm

Doubek, A. (2021, September 21). *50 Best Shadow Work Journal Prompts For Mental Health And Healing.* Dancing through the Rain. https://dancingthroughtherain.com/shadow-work-journal-prompts/

Earley, J. (2009). *Self-therapy: A step-by-step guide to creating inner wholeness using IFS, a new, cutting edge psychotherapy.* Mill City Press.

Emerson, R. W. (2013). In *The Power of the Heart: Loving the self.* Createspace Independent Publishing Platform.

Gandhi, M. K. (2009). In *God makes the rivers to flow: An anthology of the world's Sacred Poetry & Prose.* Nilgiri Press.

Green, K. (2014, November). *Healing the Effects of Trauma with Shadow Work. Shadow Work.* https://shadow-work.com/healing-effects-trauma-shadow-work/

Integrative Life Center. (2021, August 16). *Signs of Repressed Childhood Trauma in Adults.* https://integrativelifecenter.com/wellness-blog/signs-of-repressed-child-hood-trauma-in-adults/

Jacobson, S. (2015a, November 17). *The Power of Personal Values - Are You Missing Out?* Harley Therapy Blog. https://www.harleytherapy.co.uk/counselling/personal-values-know-yours.htm

Jacobson, S. (2015b, October 13). *Negative Thinking – Is It Sabotaging Your Life?* Harley Therapy Blog. https://www.harleytherapy.co.uk/counselling/negative-think-ing.htm

Jacobson, S. (2016, May 10). *Self Sabotage – What it Looks Like and Why You Do it*. Harley Therapy Blog. https://www.harleytherapy.co.uk/counselling/self-sabo-tage.htm

Jacobson, S. (2017a, March 23). *What is the "Inner Child"?* Harley Therapy Blog. https://www.harleytherapy.-co.uk/counselling/what-is-the-inner-child.htm

Jacobson, S. (2017b, March 28). *Inner Child Work - What Is It and Can You Benefit?* Harley Therapy Blog. https://www.harleytherapy.co.uk/counselling/inner-child-work-can-benefit.htm

Jacobson, S. (2018a, April 26). *What is Reparenting?* Harley Therapy Blog. https://www.harleytherapy.co.uk/coun-selling/what-is-reparenting.htm

Jacobson, S. (2018b, September 25). *Reparenting Yourself - How to Heal the Mother Wound*. Harley Therapy Blog. https://www.harleytherapy.co.uk/counselling/reparenting-yourself-how-to-heal-the-mother-wound.htm

Jacobson, S. (2019a, June 4). T*he Real Reason Your Self Worth is Low - and How to Fix It.* Harley Therapy Blog. https://www.harleytherapy.co.uk/counselling/low-self-worth.htm

Jacobson, S. (2019b, January 17). *A Sense of Self - How Important Is It to Know Who You Are?* Harley Therapy Blog. https://www.harleytherapy.co.uk/counselling/a-sense-of-self-who-am-i.htm

Jacobson, S. (n.d.). *Fear of Abandonment - 12 Signs it is Secretly Sabotaging Your Relationships.* Harley Therapy Blog. Retrieved December 22, 2021, from https://www.harleytherapy.co.uk/counselling/fear-of-aban-donment.htm

Jeffrey, S. (2014a, August 13). *Shadow Work: A Complete Guide to Getting to Know Your Darker Half.* CEOsage. https://scottjeffrey.com/shadow-work/#Five_Benefit-s_of_Jungian_Shadow_Work

Jeffery, S. (2014b, June 4). *7 Steps to Discovering Your Personal Core Values.* CEOsage. https://scottjeffrey.com/per-sonal-core-values/

Jeffrey, S. (2017a, May 15). *Archetypes: A Practical Guide to Inner Work Using Archetypes.* CEOsage. https://scottjeffrey.com/archetypes-psychology/#Archetype-s_A_Doorway_to_Knowing_Yourself

Jeffrey, S. (2017b, November 7). *Meditation Guidance and Instructions for Effective Mind Training.* CEOsage. https://scottjeffrey.com/meditation-guidance-instructions/

Jeffrey, S. (2017c, January 31). *How to Ground Yourself: 9 Powerful Grounding Techniques.* CEOsage. https://scottjef-frey.com/how-to-ground-yourself/

Jeffrey, S. (2018, January 1). *Hero's Journey Steps: 10 Stages to Joseph Campbell's Monomyth.* Scott Jeffrey. https://scottjeffrey.com/heros-journey-steps/#The_Heros_Journey_in_Drama

Jeffrey, S. (2019, April 20). *15 Self Awareness Activities and Exercises to Build Emotional Intelligence*. CEOsage. https://scottjeffrey.com/self-awareness-activities-exercises/

Johnson, R. A. (1992). *Inner Work: Using dreams and active imagination for personal growth*. Harper San Francisco.

Johnson, R. A. (1994). *Owning Your Own Shadow: Understanding the dark side of the psyche*. Harper San Francisco.

Jung, C. G. (1960). Structure & Dynamics of the Psyche. In G. Adler & R. Hull (Eds.), *The Collected Works of C. G. Jung* (Vol. 8). Princeton University Press.

Jung, C. G. (1966). Two Essays on Analytical Psychology. In H. Howard, M. Fordham, & G. Adler (Eds.), & R. F. C. Hull (Trans.), *The Collected Works of C. G. Jung* (Vol. 7). Routledge & K. Paul.

Jung, C. G. (1967). Alchemical Studies. In *The Collected Works of C. G. Jung* (Vol. 13). Routledge & Kegan Paul.

Jung, C. G. (1970). Psychology and Religion: West and East. In G. Adler & R. F. C. Hull (Eds.), *The Collected Works of C. G. Jung* (Vol. 11). Princeton University Press.

Jung, C. G. (1980). Psychology and Alchemy. In G. Adler & R. F. C. Hull (Trans.), *The Collected Works of C. G. Jung* (Vol. 12). Princeton University Press.

King, M. L. (1968, April 3). *I've Been to the Mountaintop* [Speech]. https://speakola.com/ideas/martin-luther-king-jr-ive-been-to-the-mountaintop-1968

Lavers, C. (2020). *Shadow Work: A simple guide*. Christina Lavers Coaching. https://www.christinalaverscoaching.com/shadow-work.php

Lindberg, S. (2018, September 14). *Projection in Psychology: Definition, Defense Mechanism, Example*s. Healthline.

https://www.healthline.com/health/projection-psychology#defense-mechanism

My Spiritual Shenanigans. (2020, April 18). *7 Effective Journaling Ideas for Self-Healing.* https://myspiritualshenanigans.blog/5-journaling-ideas-self-healing/

Oprah Winfrey Network. (2012). Debbie Ford's Forgiveness Meditation: SuperSoul Sunday [Video]. In *Youtube.* https://www.youtube.com/watch?v=7RZ2XPw8-gU

Pharaon, V. (n.d.). *Your Beautiful Life.*

Raypole, C. (2021, September 9). *8 Tips for Healing Your Inner Child.* Healthline. https://www.healthline.com/health/mental-health/inner-child-healing#acknowledge

Rhodes, J. (2009, April 20). *How To Do Automatic Writing.* MindPerk. http://www.mindperk.com/articles/how-to-do-automatic-writing/

Roberts, G., & Machon, A. (Eds.). (2015). *Appreciative Healthcare Practice: A guide to compassionate, person-centered care.* M & K Publishing.

Schultz, D. P., & Schultz, S. E. (2017). *Theories of personality* (11th ed.). Cengage Learning.

Shadow Work Seminars. (2021). *The 12 Shadow Types.* Shadow Types. https://shadowtypes.com/home/about-the-12-shadow-types/

Stevens, A. (1999). *On Jung: An updated edition with a reply to Jung's critics.* Princeton University Press.

Stines, S. (2017, April 30). *Writing Prompts for Recovery from an Abusive/Toxic Relationship.* Psych Central. https://psychcentral.com/pro/recovery-expert/2017/04/writing-prompts-for-recovery-from-an-abusivetoxic-relationship#1

Stone, H., & Stone, S. (1993). *Embracing Your Inner Critic: Turning self-criticism into a creative asset.* Harper.

TEDx Talks. (2018). Give Your Inner Child Permission to Heal. In *YouTube*. https://www.youtube.com/watch?v=uKHkq6S3kaU

Thatcher, T. (2018, November 20). *Healing Childhood Trauma in Adults*. Highland Springs. https://highland-springsclinic.org/blog/healing-childhood-trauma-adults/

Tropeaka. (2019, September 19). *30 Days of Journal Prompts for Reflection and Self-Discovery*. https://tropeaka.com.au/blogs/the-latest/30-days-of-journal-prompts-for-reflection-and-self-discovery

Vinney, C. (2021). *What Is a Projection Defense Mechanism?* Verywell Mind. https://www.verywellmind.com/what-is-a-projection-defense-mechanism-5194898

von Franz, M.-L. (1978). The Process of Individuation. In C. G. Jung (Ed.), *Man and His Symbols* (pp. 158–229). Anchor Press.

West, M. (n.d.). *Complexes and Archetypes*. Society of Analytical Psychology. Retrieved December 8, 2021, from https://www.thesap.org.uk/resources/articles-on-jungian-psychology-2/about-analysis-and-therapy/complexes-and-archetypes/

Wikipedia Contributors. (2019, March 22). *Carl Jung*. Wikipedia. https://en.wikipedia.org/wiki/Carl_Jung

Williams, S. (1868). *Twilight hours, a legacy of verse*. Strahan & co.

Young- Eisendrath, P., & Dawson, T. (Eds.). (2008). *The Cambridge Companion to Jung* (2nd ed.). Cambridge University Press.

Zimberoff, D. (2017, July 22). *Discovering Jungian Shadows and the Autonomous Complexes*. Wellness Institute Blog. https://web.wellness-institute.org/blog/discovering-jungian-shadows-and-the-autonomous-complexes

Printed in Great Britain
by Amazon

16402360R00092